UNIVERSITY OF NORTH CAROLINA AT CHAPEL HILL
DEPARTMENT OF ROMANCE LANGUAGES

NORTH CAROLINA STUDIES IN THE ROMANCE LANGUAGES AND LITERATURES

Founder: URBAN TIGNER HOLMES
Editor: STIRLING HAIG

Distributed by:

UNIVERSITY OF NORTH CAROLINA PRESS
CHAPEL HILL
North Carolina 27514
U.S.A.

NORTH CAROLINA STUDIES IN THE
ROMANCE LANGUAGES AND LITERATURES
Number 219

ABYSMAL GAMES
IN THE
NOVELS OF SAMUEL BECKETT

ABYSMAL GAMES

IN THE

NOVELS OF SAMUEL BECKETT

BY

ANGELA B. MOORJANI

CHAPEL HILL

NORTH CAROLINA STUDIES IN THE ROMANCE
LANGUAGES AND LITERATURES
U.N.C. DEPARTMENT OF ROMANCE LANGUAGES

1982

Library of Congress Cataloging in Publication Data

Moorjani, Angela B.
  Abysmal games in the novels of Samuel Beckett.

  (North Carolina studies in the Romance languages and literatures; no. 219.)
  Bibliography: p.
  1. Beckett, Samuel, 1906-   — Fictional works. 2. Beckett, Samuel, 1906-   — Technique. I. Title. II. Series.

PR6003.E282Z7815   1982   843'.914   82-17641
ISBN 0-8078-9223-8

I. S. B. N. 84-499-5915-2

DEPÓSITO LEGAL: V. 2.180 - 1982

ARTES GRÁFICAS SOLER, S. A. - LA OLIVERETA, 28 - VALENCIA (18) - 1982

To Kishin

CONTENTS

Acknowledgments 11
Key to Texts Cited 13
Introduction 15
Part I: Narrative Repetition 23
Part II: Thematic Reduplication 68
Conclusion 133
Bibliography 152

ACKNOWLEDGMENTS

Permission to quote from Beckett's works has been kindly granted by the Editions de Minuit and Grove Press. Earlier versions of this book have appeared in *Samuel Beckett, The Art of Rhetoric,* edited by E. Morot-Sir, H. Harper, D. McMillan III, *L'Esprit Créateur* (Fall 1977), and *Perspectives on Contemporary Literature,* 6 (Lexington: Univ. Press of Kentucky, 1981), to the editors of which I am grateful for permission to reprint.

A summer research grant and sabbatical leave from the University of Maryland, Baltimore County helped me research this book. For assisting me in the preparation and typing of the manuscript I am indebted to Elizabeth Keller and Derryl Johnson. To them and to my colleagues in the Department of Modern Languages and Linguistics my special thanks. And finally I want to express my appreciation to Professor Edouard Morot-Sir whose encouragement and suggestions helped me on the way.

KEY TO TEXTS CITED

Beckett's works are referred to by their initial title, whether English or French. If the work was first written in French, I have cited the French text, followed immediately by its translation into English. Throughout, I have separated English translations from the original French by a slash or a line in the case of longer passages. Unless otherwise indicated, quotations in my text are followed by the page numbers referring to the Grove Press editions, if in English, and to the Editions de Minuit, if in French. The first part of the Bibliography lists the exact editions cited.

INTRODUCTION

Voices echoing echoes, images mirroring mirror images, stories embedded inside stories, myths repeating myths, these are some of the ways in which Beckett's narrative fiction subverts the order of discourse through its play with infinity. This essay, in two parts, analyzes how Beckett's novels undermine textual linearity, on the one hand, and the myths of self-transparency, on the other, by turning words into toys, writing into abysmal play.

In order to understand the intricate strategies of the Beckettian assault on narrative procedures and since, within his novels, narrative postures range from authorial glosses to direct quotes from inner voices, it is important to define the terms referring to the various quoting, narrating, and metanarrating techniques. This area of narratology has generated a number of sets of categories leading to considerable confusion among commentators.[1] The terms given below (which will be explained at the end of the list) emphasize the movement from direct to indirect quotation (anchored more or less in the character's discourse), then from quotation to narration (privileging the narrator's discourse), and from narration to glosses on narration (foregrounding the discourse as discourse). This movement also entails a progression from the mimetic to the abstract:

---

[1] For a review of narrative terminology, see Dorrit Cohn, *Transparent Minds* (Princeton: Princeton Univ. Press, 1978), pp. 3-17; and Gérard Genette, "Discours du récit," in *Figures III* (Paris: Seuil, 1972), pp. 183-203; translated by Jane E. Lewin as *Narrative Discourse* (Ithaca: Cornell Univ. Press, 1980), pp. 161-85.

I. QUOTED DISCOURSE

	MODE		QUOTED/SELF-QUOTED
	A. *Free direct style:*		Have to get out.
1. Thought	(also, "interior monologue")		"
2. Speech			"
3. Writing			"
	B. *Tagged direct style:* "I have to get out of here,"		
1. Thought	(also, "soliloquy")	"	she/I thought.
2. Speech	(also, "soliloquy")	"	she/I said.
3. Writing		"	she/I wrote.
	C. *Free indirect style:*		She/I had to get out of here.
1. Thought			"
2. Speech			"
3. Writing			"
	D. *Tagged indirect style:*		
1. Thought		She/I thought that	she/I had to get out of there.
2. Speech		She/I said that	
3. Writing		She/I wrote that	"

II. NARRATED DISCOURSE

	A. *Narrated:* She wanted to leave.	B. *Self-Narrated:*
1. Thought	(also, "psycho-narration")	I wanted to leave.
2. Speech		(also, "self-narration")
3. Writing		

III. NARRATED EVENTS

A. Showing or Scene
B. Telling or Summary

IV. METANARRATION

A. *Narrative Commentary*

1. Narration
2. Story
3. Textual Organization

B. *Embeddings and mise en abyme*

1. Narration
2. Story
3. Textual Organization

The four modes included under quoted discourse were proposed by Seymour Chatman.[2] The first of these, free direct style, quotes mental, spoken, or written discourse without any explicit introduction or quotation marks (Have to get out). In this mode, which is often elliptical, the character's point of view and discourse predominate to the exclusion of the narrator's.[3] In tagged direct style, on the other hand, the character's words are surrounded by the punctuation and tag statement of the narrator ("I have to get out of here," she said). The third mode of quoted discourse, free indirect style, is the most complex of the four. Dorrit Cohn, referring particularly to psychic description, defines it as "a character's mental discourse in the guise of the narrator's discourse."[4] That is, free indirect style involves simultaneously the character's and the narrator's point of view and mode. As in free direct style, no quotation marks or explicit remarks by the narrator introduce the character's thoughts or words. The diction (style level, word choice, and so on) as well as most spatio-temporal indications ("now," "here," but not verb tense) are anchored in the character, whereas the pronouns and verb tense are related to the narrator (She had to get out of here). And finally, in tagged indirect style, the character's discourse is quoted indirectly, is recast into the diction and deictics (pronouns, verb tense, and other spatio-temporal expressions) of the narrator (She thought that she had to get out of there). For this reason, Genette refers to this fourth category as "discours *transposé*"/"*transposed* speech."[5]

In narrated discourse, the protagonist's words and thoughts are obviously eclipsed by the narrator's (She wanted to leave at once). In his chapter on mood, Genette makes the helpful distinction between a "récit de paroles"/"narrative of words" and a "récit de

---

[2] See "The Structure of Narrative Transmission," in *Style and Structure in Literature*, ed. Roger Fowler (Ithaca: Cornell Univ. Press, 1975), p. 230.

[3] In *The Five Clocks* (New York: Harcourt Brace and World, 1967), Martin Joos points out that, in interpersonal communication, in moving from formal to consultative to casual to intimate style more and more context is taken for granted causing speech to become increasingly elliptical. Speaking to oneself or mental discourse is, of course, a step beyond intimate style.

[4] *Transparent Minds*, p. 14.

[5] "Discours du récit," pp. 191-92./*Narrative Discourse*, pp. 170-71.

pensées"/"narrative of thoughts."[6] Of the two, the technique of narrated thoughts or of a narrator's inside view of a character's mental discourse has generated particularly interesting discussion. Thus, within a third-person context, for the mode formerly known as omniscient analysis, Dorrit Cohn appropriately coined the term "psycho-narration," on the analogy of "psychoanalysis," which she defines as "the narrator's discourse about a character's consciousness," whereas she prefers the term "self-narration" (after "self-analysis") for the technique used to produce retrospective psychic discourse in first-person novels.[7] As we shall see, "self-narration" is one of the dominant narrative postures in the Beckettian novels after *Murphy*.

It is again Genette who draws attention to the difference between narrated discourse and narrated events. At the same time, he points out that, of the two types of narrated events, dramatization — showing — reenforces the illusion of mimesis, whereas summary — telling — corresponds to *diegesis* or pure narrative, the category that Plato in Book III of *The Republic* contrasted with mimesis.[8]

The following passage from Beckett's *Murphy* will serve to illustrate some of the narrative techniques outlined so far. I have indicated the modes in brackets:

> He heard her rise and go to the window, then come and stand at the foot of the bed. So far from opening his eyes he sucked in his cheeks. [narrated events: scene] Was she perhaps subject to feelings of compassion? [quoted thoughts: free indirect style]
>
> "I'll tell you what more you can do," she said.... [quoted words: tagged direct style]
>
> The gentle passion. [quoted thoughts: free direct style or "interior monologue"] Murphy lost all his yellow again. [narrated events: summary] (p. 38)

---

[6] "Discours du récit," pp. 189-91./*Narrative Discourse*, pp. 169-71.

[7] *Transparent Minds*, p. 14. See also the chapters entitled "Psycho-Narration," pp. 21-57; and "Retrospective Techniques," pp. 143-72.

[8] "Discours du récit," pp. 184-91 ff./*Narrative Discourse*, pp. 162-71 ff. For an extended discussion of "showing" versus "telling," see Wayne C. Booth, *The Rhetoric of Fiction* (Chicago: Univ. of Chicago Press, 1961).

INTRODUCTION 19

The following passage also from *Murphy* is not as easily analyzed, however:

> The story that Miss Carridge had to tell was very pathetic and tedious....
> "He gets out his razor to shave, as he always did regular about noon." A lie. The old boy shaved once a week and then the last thing at night. "That I do know, because I found the brush on the dresser with a squeeze of paste on top." A lie.... (p. 144)

This scene is one of Beckett's early attacks on mimetic illusion by means of two of his favorite narrative strategies, embedded narration, on the one hand, and a negating metanarrative voice, on the other. Both are ways of commenting on the text as it is being produced. Thus, Miss Carridge's story about the "old boy's" suicide, accidental according to her, is staged as a narrative of events within a narrative of events. As a consequence, the sentence, "'He gets out his razor...'," functions on two levels, as the directly quoted speech of a character within the novel, and as a narrated event within the character's story. The subsequent comments, "A lie. The old boy shaved once a week..." are therefore difficult to tag. Whose words are they? The novel's omniscient narrator's who knows all about the "old boy" and the thoughts and words of the teller of the story too? Or are they the directly quoted thoughts of Miss Carridge contradicting her own tale as she is telling it?

The narrating is further undermined by the next group of sentences. The detail of the brush with the paste, which is intended to add to the verisimilitude of the scene, is demolished as a lie on top of a lie, or as an example of a narrator being carried away by her fiction. It is, in fact, just such realistic details that often mark stories as fiction or lies.[9] Since it is clearly *Murphy*'s omniscient narrator who disrupts the rest of his character's story, for example with the description of her pronunciation of "seizure": "Pronounced on the analogy of manure" (p. 145), thus once again drawing attention to the telling process, one is inclined to attribute

---

[9] See Roland Barthes, "L'Effet de réel," *Communications*, 11 (1968), pp. 84-89.

the negating of the story as a lie (repeated four times) to this voice as well. The narrator's comments subvert the embedded narrator's discourse and by implication the mimetic illusion of fiction as such.

It is clear that what makes this passage difficult to analyze is the narrative stepping in and out of several levels of discourse. In order to distinguish among these levels, the word "narration" is used for the act of telling (in this sense comprising narrated discourse and events), whereas the term "metanarration" refers to the narrative commentary on the telling, as exemplified above by the repeated, "A lie." Based on the distinction made in semantics between object language and metalanguage, that is, between a language used to discuss objects in the world and a language used to discuss language, the narration/metanarration distinction is further related to Gregory Bateson's analysis of the metacommunicative function, that is, of messages that label or frame other messages, for instance, as play, or a lie, or fiction.[10] In the sense that "metalanguage" suffices for comments on the different levels of language — phonology, morphology, syntax, and semantics — and "metacommunication" for the varied labeling of messages, I believe the term "metanarration" will do for narrative descriptions of both telling and told.[11] Metanarration foregrounds

---

[10] See Bateson's "A Theory of Play and Fantasy" (1955); rpt. in *Steps to an Ecology of Mind* (New York: Ballantine Books, 1972), pp. 177-93. Bateson bases his discussion of the metacommunicative function on the earlier work of Whitehead, Russell, Wittgenstein, Carnap, and Whorf. He refers particularly to Russell's resolution of logical and semantic paradoxes by his hierachy of types, that is, by distinguishing among different levels of classes and stipulating that no class can be a member of itself. See Russell's *The Principles of Mathematics*, 2nd ed. (New York: W. W. Norton, 1938), pp. 523-28; and Alfred N. Whitehead and Bertrand Russell, *Principia Mathematica*, I, 2nd ed. (1925; rpt. Cambridge, Eng.: Univ. Press, Paperback Edition to *56, 1962), pp. 37-65. For further discussion of the relation between Russell's theory of logical types and metalanguage or the "levels of language" doctrine, see Irving M. Copi, *The Theory of Logical Types* (London: Routledge and Kegan Paul, 1971), pp. 197-14.

[11] In her *Structure de la Trilogie de Beckett* (The Hague: Mouton, 1976), p. 19, Dina Sherzer uses the two words "méta-narration" and "méta-récit" to refer to comments on the narration and comments on the story respectively. She also points out the similarity between such metatextual comments and Booth's category of the "self-conscious narrator," in *Rhetoric of Fiction*, p. 155. I have preferred to collapse her two terms

both the narrative fiction and the narrating process as writing or text, that is, it stages discourse as discourse.

The ways in which embedded narratives function as metanarrative commentary on the text are analyzed by Genette.[12] In his discussion of narrative levels, Genette traces the technique of what he terms "récit au second degré" or "récit *métadiégétique*"/ "second-degree narrative" or "*metadiegetic* narrative" back to the *Odyssey* and other epics, mentions its importance for the composition of the *Thousand and One Nights,* and shows how, after the adoption of the technique by the novel in the seventeenth century, embedded narratives appear in such eighteenth-century novels as *Manon Lescaut* and *Tristram Shandy,* in the nineteenth-century novels *Sarrasine* and *Wuthering Heights,* among others, and the twentieth-century *A la recherche du temps perdu* and the New Novel. Genette outlines three ways in which an embedded narrative comments on the narratives that contain it. The narratives can be related by (1) a causative link, the second narrative serving to explain the first; (2) a thematic relation, the narratives being analogous or antithetical; and (3) the embedded narrative can serve to obstruct or distract as in the *Thousand and One Nights.* According to Genette, abysmal structure is a special instance of the second category: it consists of an analogous relation between narratives pushed to the limits of near identity.

In his *Récit spéculaire,* Lucien Dällenbach points out that an embedded fragment can function simultaneously as interior duplication and metacommentary.[13] Dällenbach in turn divides *mise en abyme* into three categories: (1) simple reduplication (a fragment which resembles the work that contains it); (2) infinite reduplication (an embedded fragment containing in turn a fragment, and so on); and (3) "réduplication aporistique" or paradoxical reduplication (a fragment supposedly containing the work which contains it).[14] Miss Carridge's narrative, the fragment embedded

---

into one. Sherzer relates her categories to Roman Jakobson's discussion of the metalinguistic function, which can be found in his "Closing Statements: Linguistics and Poetics," in *Style in Language,* ed. Thomas A. Sebeok (Cambridge, Mass.: MIT Press, 1960), pp. 350-77.

[12] "Discours du récit," pp. 238-43./*Narrative Discourse,* pp. 227-34.
[13] *Le Récit spéculaire* (Paris: Seuil, 1977), p. 76.
[14] *Le Récit spéculaire,* p. 51.

in *Murphy*, is an instance of simple reduplication, whereas, as we shall see, it is infinite reduplication which is Beckett's preferred abysmal game. It is Dällenbach too who specifies that *mise en abyme* can variously reflect (1) the narration, (2) the story, and (3) the textual organization.[15] *Murphy*'s fragment, discussed above, doubles the narration, the character's way of telling the story mirroring by implication the narrator's. All three types, however, are found at work simultaneously in Beckett's novels.

In this essay, although I will review and add to the critical discussions of the ways in which Beckett perturbs the textual surface of his novels by word play and negating glosses, and comment on how he draws attention to the textuality of the writing, I will concentrate on what has not been analyzed to date, that is, the intricate game strategies that turn each text into abysmal play. The first part will concentrate on narrative reduplication, on the repetition of mirror and echo games, the second on thematic *mise en abyme* and the undoing of mythic antinomies.

---

[15] *Le récit spéculaire*, p. 61 ff.

PART I

NARRATIVE REPETITION

Beckett's play with narrative structure spans his entire writing career. The early writings mockingly contest classical narrative modes, the works from *Watt* onward playfully deconstruct them. In the pre-*Watt* fiction, with few exceptions, the third-person narrators undermine linear form and authorial point of view by subverting the story-line and slipping at least once out of their sovereign anonymity into a first-person proximity to the protagonist. The character is but my other self, a mirror image, the narrators imply. A particularly playful instance of such an encounter between implicit author, narrator, and protagonist occurs in "Dream of Fair to Middling Women." In this unfinished novel of the thirties, in which both the narrator and protagonist mock the author face to face, we find an early example of double narrative self-reflexivity: " 'Behold, Mr. Beckett,' said [Belacqua] whitely, 'a dud mystic.' ... Guardedly, reservedly, we beheld him ... face to face, even as he sometimes contrived to behold himself."[1] Similarly, in *More Pricks than Kicks,* the collection of short stories published in 1934, the narrator explains that his information comes from the character: "I know all this because he told me. We were

---

[1] Quoted by John Fletcher from the unpublished "Dream of Fair to Middling Women," in *The Novels of Samuel Beckett* (London: Chatto and Windus, 1964), p. 28.

I have adopted the term "implied" or "implicit" author from Wayne C. Booth, *Rhetoric of Fiction,* pp. 71-76 and p. 151 ff. Booth describes the "implied author" as an implicit second self the author stages in the novel and stresses that this narrative pose is not to be confused with the actual person of the writer.

Pylades and Orestes for a period..." (p. 37). "My little internus homo," is how the narrator describes Belacqua — whose name itself suggests a mirror — a little further on. Thus, the mirror of realistic fiction has become an inner glass in which the narrator hopes to come face to face with himself. Indeed, Beckett had praised such inward turning, the tendency of much of twentieth-century fiction, in his 1931 essay on Proust.[2] Finally, though, the narrator's narcissistic project ends in failure, for the image in the mirror is rejected: "He [Belacqua] was an impossible person in the end. I gave him up in the end because he was not *serious*" (p. 38).

In *Murphy*, written shortly after the Belacqua stories and published in 1938, the narrator at first adopts the posture of authorial sovereignty. He casts himself in the role of a puppet master who pulls the strings of his characters and maneuvers them through circular repetitions that mimic the patterns of the universe. On the other hand, Murphy is not a puppet, the narrator informs the reader on page 122. Instead, that the protagonist holds the privileged position of inner persona is made explicit in Chapter vi. In this famous chapter, the narrator explains that his description of Murphy's mind will not correspond to reality, thus attacking the conventions of narrative omniscience, but will be limited to how that mind views itself, for "Murphy's mind is after all the gravamen of these informations" (p. 107). Locating narrative perspective within Murphy's psyche, then, Chapter vi is an example of triple narrative point of view, that is, within the frame of the metanarrative voice commenting on the "painful duty" (p. 113) of describing Murphy's mind, both a third-person narrative voice and the protagonist's voice are present, causing the text to waver between the modes of psycho-narration (omniscient thought description) and free indirect quotation of the character's mental discourse.[3]

---

[2] For a summary of the theories on the inward turn of narrative fiction, see Dorrit Cohn, *Transparent Minds*, pp. 6-9 ff.

[3] Much of Chapter vi consists of psycho-narration, beginning with: "Murphy's mind pictured itself as a large hollow sphere, hermetically closed to the universe without" (p. 107). This omniscient analysis (framed by metanarrative comments) periodically gives way to free indirect quotations of Murphy's own mental discourse, as for example, "But where then

Unlike earlier examples of such shifts in narrative perspective, in Flaubert's novels, for instance, in which they occur unobtrusively, in *Murphy*, as we have seen, the third-person narrator self-consciously glosses his textual maneuvers. Indeed, since he plays one narrative strategy against the other, authorial omniscience against inward turning self-transparency, he necessarily transgresses and ridicules the conventions of each mode. On the one hand, *Murphy*'s third-person narrator undermines his posture of impartial observer by drawing attention to the process of narrating — "The above passage is carefully calculated to deprave the cultivated reader" (p. 118) — and by self-consciously trading his stance of puppeteer for that of an inner persona's confidant. On the other hand, the contention that Murphy is the source of narrative perspective is flagrantly contradicted in several ways. First of all, though many outer and inner events are described from Murphy's point of view, there are entire chapters (iv, vii, and x) in which narrative perspective shifts with comic speed from one minor character to the other. And, of course, Chapters xii and xiii follow the protagonist's death. (Similarly, the Belacqua stories had continued after the persona's death.) In addition, the narrative comment at the beginning of Chapter vii blatantly contradicts the primacy of Murphy's point of view: "The encounter, on which so much unhinges, between Murphy and Ticklepenny, took place on Friday, October the 11th (though Murphy did not know that)..." (p. 114).

The narrator thus fails to maintain narrative continuity in either mode. The posture of omnipotence is comically undermined, the character as other self denied. Thus, for the progressive consonance between narrator and protagonist found in such third-person novels as *Le Rouge et le noir*, *Madame Bovary*, and *A Portrait of the Artist as a Young Man*, *Murphy* substitutes a progressive dissonance. Although the biography of Beckett points to certain autobiographical strains in Belacqua and Murphy, Beckett's early fiction backs away from an identification between narrator and character, moves from consonance to dissonance.

---

was the supreme Caress?" (p. 109), and the third from the last paragraph of the Chapter: "It was pleasant to kick the Ticklepennies and Miss Carridges simultaneously together into ghastly acts of love.... So pleasant that pleasant was not the word" (pp. 112-13).

Why this is so, *Watt*, the enigmatic novel written in the early forties, will make clear.

In *Watt*, Beckett's testing of clashing narrative procedures results in a narrative structure that has puzzled readers ever since. Indeed, since no beginning, end, or continuity can be assigned to the text, only a non-linear reading is able to account for the novel's horizontal and vertical repetitions and discontinuities.[4] Of the two, the horizontal discontinuity is most immediately apparent, for *Watt* is an unfinished novel whose fragments are punctuated with "Hiatus in MS" and question marks, indicating suspensions. Finally, the addenda of important material the narrator failed to incorporate clearly underscore the novel's incompleteness.

Similarly, on the narrative level, the text moves vertically from the all-knowing to an unknowing position. In the first and fourth parts of this four-part novel, an unnamed narrator writes from the omniscient perspective. In the first twenty-four pages of the novel, however, most perceptions are projected through Mr Hackett, a double of both the narrator and Watt: the unqualifiable Watt appears to Hackett — the play on Beckett's name becomes obvious — in the manner characters fade into a narrator's conciousness.[5] At first, Watt dissolves into the gray background: he could be man, woman, or parcel. Mysteriously intrigued by this impersonal, asexual apparition, Mr Hackett seeks to determine its identity or civil status: "Nationality, family, birthplace, confession, occupation,

---

[4] In "Ariadne's Thread: Repetition and the Narrative Line," *Critical Inquiry*, 3 (Autumn 1976), 68, J. Hillis Miller writes: "The image of the line cannot, it is easy to see, be detached from the problem of repetition. Repetition might be defined as anything which happens to the line to trouble or even to confound its straightforward linearity: returnings, knottings, recrossings, crinklings to and fro, suspensions, interruptions, fictionalizings."

[5] Mathew Winston — "*Watt's* First Footnote," *Journal of Modern Literature*, 6, No. 1 (1977), 71-72 — points out that the omission of the customary period after Mr. and Mrs. in *Watt* serves to blur the outlines of the characters. Or is it just a matter of British versus American usage?

In *Le Récit spéculaire*, p. 101 f., Lucien Dällenbach mentions three ways in which authors mirror themselves in their works' narrators. Authors can suggest similarity by means of (a) professions or activities resembling their own, (b) a "nom à clé" or disguised name, and (c) a name evoking the name found on the title page. Beckett uses these strategies among others, as we shall see.

means of existence, distinctive signs, you cannot be in ignorance of all this" (p. 21). At the same time, the relation between Hackett and Watt, between narrator and character, is perceived as one of identity. Mr Nixon, speaking of Watt, tells Mr Hackett: "The curious thing is... that when I see him, or think of him, I think of you, and that when I see you, or think of you, I think of him" (p. 19). So that the narrator's desire to circumscribe the unknown character impinging onto his consciousness posits a subjectivity transparent to itself. It is this position — together with other absolutes — that the novel will demolish. Consequently, Mr Hackett, a figure of the illusory, all-knowing subject, disappears from the text at the beginning of Watt's story. He has learned next to nothing about his persona; undifferentiated darkness seeps over his horizon: "Now it was quite dark. Yes, now the western sky was as the eastern, which was as the southern, which was as the northern" (p. 24).

On the other hand, the reader learns in the second and third parts of the novel that Watt's story is not told by one narrator, but is recounted by Sam as told to him by Watt, who narrates the quest by an earlier self. (Watt tells the story to Sam who writes it down in his notebook and then transcribes it into narrative discourse.) Consequently, since Parts I and IV imply an omnicient perspective, Sam's narrative about how the story came to be written, inscribed within the novel's fictional frame,[6] presupposes a series of embedded narrators: on one end, the implicit author of *Watt*, of whom Hackett is a double; then Sam, who writes Watt's story in the third person and the Sam-Watt relationship in the first; followed by Watt, the first-person narrator of his journey to and from Knott's. Three transcriptions are implied. The vertical chain, however, stretches even further, since in one direction, the names of the narrators — Hackett (third-person) and Sam (first-person) — evoke the author of the title page,

---

[6] Lucien Dällenbach ("Le Récit du récit," in *Le Récit spéculaire*, pp. 119-22) indicates several works which inscribe within themselves the narrative's own story, among others, the eleventh-century *Vie de saint Alexis*, and the novels of Cervantes, Laclos, Jean-Paul, and more recently, Proust. See also J. Hillis Millier's description ("Ariadne's Thread," p. 74) of how a novel "deconstructs itself in the process of constructing its web of storytelling."

and since in the other direction, while Sam listens to Watt, Watt in turn listens to an inner, unidentifiable voice: "Watt spoke as one speaking to dictation, or reciting, parrot-like, a text, by long repetition become familiar" (p. 156). And the question imposes itself about what this most distant text of the series transcribes and so on indefinitely.

In "Freud et la scène de l'écriture," Jacques Derrida describes Freud's writing machine metaphor for the psychic apparatus in terms of just such a system of stratified writing. Of the unconscious text in this system he writes that it is "déjà tissé de traces pures, de différences où s'unissent le sens et la force, texte nulle part présent, constitué d'archives qui sont *toujours déjà* des transcriptions."/"The unconscious text is already woven of pure traces, differences in which meaning and force are united; a text nowhere present, consisting of archives which are *always already* transcriptions."[7]

Resembling such psychic archives, *Watt*'s embedded narrative series can thus be schematized as follows:

(Samuel Beckett, named on the title page as the author of *Watt*)

    (The third-person narrator, the implicit author of the novel's metanarrative and omniscient frame)

        (Sam, the third-person narrator of Watt's story, the first-person narrator of his relation to Watt)

            (Watt, the first-person narrator of his past quest)

                (The voice from which Watt quotes)

                    (The voice from which the voice

---

[7] *L'Ecriture et la différence* (Paris: Seuil, 1967), p. 314. Jeffrey Mehlman's translation can be found in *Yale French Studies*, No. 48 (1972), p. 92.

> from which
> Watt quotes
> is quoting)
>
> and
> so
> on

From these uncertain sources, then, the text surfaces badly tattered into the torn fabric of the novel. For up through the series, the quoted text is inaccurately heard, transmitted, and recorded. Of Watt's inarticulate murmur, Sam explains, "much fell in vain on my imperfect hearing and understanding, and much by the rushing wind was carried away, and lost for ever" (p. 156). If the narrator on one end of the series could adequately hear and transmit the voice on the other, the text would assure a continuous discourse, the total possession of self. Indeed, Derrida has described the voice listening to itself as the major instance of such illusory self-transcendence.[8] But in *Watt*, instead of total discourse, the narrators transmit from one polyphonous level to the text, a fading murmur heard imperfectly.

Besides pointing out the gaps in their texts, the narrators subvert them by further metanarrative critiques. The omniscient narrator introduces several footnotes into the text that negate the narrative discourse as it is being produced. Mathew Winston has shown, for example, how the novel's first footnote — "Much valuable space has been saved, in this work, that would otherwise have been lost, by avoidance of the plethoric reflexive pronoun after *say*" (p. 8) — which is a metanarrative comment on the following sentence, "Tired of waiting for the tram, said (1) Mr Hackett, they strike up an acquaintance" (p. 8), together with other footnotes and interruptions, call on the reader "to think about the book as a self-conscious fiction which reflects on the arbitrariness of its own nature and techniques."[9] Even more damaging to fictional

---

[8] *La Voix et le phénomène* (Paris: P. U. F., 1967); translated as *Speech and Phenomena* (Evanston: Northwestern Univ. Press, 1973).

[9] "*Watt*'s First Footnote," p. 71. Winston, however, believes that Sam is the writer of the footnotes as well as of the entire text, leaving questions about the frame's omniscient point of view unanswered.

It is interesting to note that the sentence — "Tired of waiting for the

verisimilitude are the much discussed footnotes in Part II: "Haemophilia is, like enlargment [sic] of the prostate, an exclusively male disorder. But not in this work" (p. 102); and "The figures given here are incorrect. The consequent calculations are therefore doubly erroneous" (p. 104).[10] (The reference to "this work" makes me attribute these interventions to the omniscient narrator-author.) And Sam, in turn, undermines his transcription of a written record of Watt's story, together with Watt's telling of it, by stating that Watt may have omitted things that happened and put in others that never took place and that he (Sam) may likewise have "left out some of the things that Watt told me, or foisted in others that Watt never told me, though I was most careful to note down all at the time, in my little notebook" (p. 126). And, as we shall see later on, the accuracy of the stories told within Watt's story is equally denied.

The novel stages not only a polyphony of narrative voices, however, but multiple visual reflections as well. Like the echoing narrative voices, a series of inner mirror images reflect each other infinitely. Sam, the central narrator, and Watt, his persona, inhabit a mental asylum, one of Beckett's images of interiority. Although at one time Sam and Watt formed a unity, meeting in the same garden, after Watt's transfer to another pavilion Sam insists on the interval between their two regions, for he says, "we had no common garden any more" (p. 164). What had been joined has become disjointed. Sam's words clearly locate the meeting with Watt within the narrator's psyche: "Continuing my inspection, like one deprived of his senses, I observed, with a distinctness that left no room for doubt, in the adjoining garden whom do you think but Watt, advancing backwards towards me" (p. 159). The key words, "inspection," "senses," "distinctness," "doubt," bring

---

tram, said (1) Mr Hackett, they strike up an acquaintance" (p. 8) — is an example of a thought soliloquy in the form of a speech soliloquy with the quotes and the reflexive pronoun omitted, since, throughout *Watt*, mental discourse is heard as an inner voice indefinable as "oneself."

[10] For interesting discussions of the footnotes on pp. 102 and 104, see Richard Ohmann, "Speech, Action, and Style," in *Literary Style*, ed. Seymour Chatman (New York: Oxford Univ. Press, 1971), pp. 241-59; Seymour Chatman, "The Structure of Narrative Transmission," pp. 226-29; and Susan Stewart, *Nonsense* (Baltimore: Johns Hopkins Univ. Press, 1978), pp. 74-75 ff.

to mind the introspective path of Descartes to the *cogito*. The narrator, in pursuit of his alienated image, seeks to recover the original proximity to self. Instead of finding his other self, however, Sam comes face to face with his own mortality. Watt, the image seen as in a mirror, takes on the signs of the dying Christ painted by Bosch, thus reversing the desired "I am what I am" to "I am what is dying."

On the level of narration, then, it is clear that Sam is either narrating psychic events (his meetings with Watt in the asylum garden) or quoting an inner discourse (Watt's story). At times Watt's discourse is quoted directly, at other times indirectly, and at still other times it appears in the guise of psycho-narration. All these modes, however, are only disguises, since it becomes obvious in Part III that the various narrative stances are only the multiple masks of an infinite self-quoted and self-narrated inner text.

That Watt is Sam's inverted mirror image is apparent not only on the visual but also on the verbal level: "As Watt walked, so now he talked, back to front" (p. 164). Thus, Watt recounts to Sam the second and final period of his stay at Knott's by inverting the sounds in the words, the words in the sentences, the sentences in a group, and then permutating the permutations. That this is an exaggerated form of word play rather than the disordered speech of a schizophrenic, as some critics have supposed, is made clear in the text.[11] Indeed, Watt's verbal permutations resemble the innumerable varieties of disguised speech that children and adults produce to keep secret what they don't want outsiders to understand. In this manner, Watt's radically disguised speech underlines the novel's contention that all language is disguise, that Watt must remain an enigma for Sam, that the self listening to the self within hears only a garbled text.

Furthermore, the anagrammes, metaplasm, and metathesis on the lexical level, the ellipsis, hyperbaton, and inversion on the

---

[11] In *Samuel Beckett: A New Approach* (New York: Dodd, Mead, and Co., 1970), p. 24, G. C. Barnard considers Watt's inversions "perfectly sound examples of schizophrenic speech-disorders." Barnard denies the similarity between Watt's speech and secret languages, since schizophrenic speech is "a compulsive spontaneous action on the part of the patient" as contrasted with the conscious manipulations of secret languages. However, that Watt's inversions depend on esthetic judgment will be emphasized by Sam's narrative comments.

syntactic level, practiced by Watt, have a long history in rhetorical theory and shock here only because taken to the extreme. Indeed, after Watt's first syntactic inversion, Sam gives a striking rhetorical analysis of Watt's inverted speech as poetic (not schizophrenic) production:

> From this it will perhaps be suspected:
> ... ...
> that the inversion was imperfect;
> that ellipse was frequent;
> that euphony was a preoccupation;
> that spontaneity was perhaps not absent;
> that there was perhaps more than a reversal of discourse;
> that the thought was perhaps inverted. (p. 164)

Sam further comments that Watt carried through the inversion of "letters" in the work "with all his usual discretion and sense of what was acceptable to the ear, and aesthetic judgement" (p. 165). [12] By insisting on esthetically arranged patterns of sound that pay no thought to habitual sound/sense relationships and by connecting language inversion to logical inversion, Sam's commentary links Watt's word games to other attacks on meaning in the novel.

And finally, the beginning of Part IV informs the reader that in addition to permutating sounds, words, and sentences, Watt inverted the parts of the story, having told part two before part one, part four before part three. Thus, Sam, the central narrator, experiences his disjunction through a disguised inner text, either scriptural or spoken, an inverted story, and an alienated image, all of which he perceives indistinctly before they fade away.

Thus, at the end of the meeting in the region between their two gardens, Watt fades from Sam's view leaving the introspection suspended: "Continuing then, when he had told me this, then he loosed my hands from his shoulders, and backwards through the hole went back, to his garden, and left me alone..." (p. 213). Again, in a continuation of the narrative chain, within Watt's story, Knott's house and garden figure a further psychic space within the narrators within narrators. Yet, whereas in Sam's narrative, the

---

[12] Since it is Watt's speech that Sam is describing, that the text reads "letters" instead of "sounds" for inversions within a word is perhaps an oversight, or else the reader is invited to imagine Sam's quoting from his notebook, an inner script.

mental asylum and garden are the place of a Cartesian quest for the *cogito*, a type of self-deification, Knott's house and garden, in Watt's narrative, are the stage of a search in medieval terms of the divine within. And although Watt "wished to see Mr Knott face to face" (p. 146), he, no more than Sam, rejoins his elusive reflection in the mirror of interiority.

That the fade-outs, both visual and auditory, are a game the narrator plays is indicated early in the novel by Watt's "little game, with the colours" (p. 39). By covering and uncovering the light of a lamp with his hat, Watt makes embers in the fireplace alternately glow and disappear until they fade to gray. By insisting that "it was no more than ... an innocent little game, to while away the time" (p. 38), the narrator underlines its importance and ambiguity. For this game of come and go is a form of the *fort/da* game discussed by Freud in *Beyond the Pleasure Principle.*

Within the context of his discussion of the compulsive repetition of unpleasant experiences, which lead him to hypothesize the death instinct, Freud recounts that the frequently reiterated activity of an eighteen-month-old child, who would throw any small object he could get hold of away from himself while uttering a contented "o-o-o-o," puzzled him until he identified it as a game. The child seemed to use all his toys only to play "gone" with them; the "o-o-o-o" sound was identified with the German word *fort*, meaning "gone." This little boy (Freud's grandson), moreover, would make one particular toy, a wooden reel with a string tied around it, disappear while uttering "o-o-o-o" and then reappear with a joyful *da* ("here"). Freud then goes on to explain the significance of the game in the following way. The little boy, who was very attached to his mother, did not cry whenever she would leave him for a few hours. Instead, symbolically substituting his toys for his mother, he played the *fort/da* game in order to master the anguishing situation of her absence. By symbolically making his mother disappear and reappear, he would seem to control the threatening situation by play. As a second interpretation, Freud adds that the child may be willfully sending his mother away, thus symbolically revenging himself for her leaving him.[13]

---

[13] See Sigmund Freud, *Beyond the Pleasure Principle* (1920), in *Standard Edition*, trans. James Strachey, XVIII (London: Hogarth Press, 1955), 14-17.

On the one hand, then, the child accomplishes the feat of symbolizing his mother by an object and then, in a further symbolization, verbalizing the painful situation of her absence. Through this symbolic process, he assumes his separateness from the mother. Yet, by making the toy (a substitute for the mother) come and go, he assures that she is not lost to him. The child thus believes in the pragmatic efficacity of symbolic play. On the other hand, the child also indentifies with the mother, imitates the mother: he does to the toy what she is doing to him. In making the toy (in this case, a substitute for himself) disappear and reappear, he convinces himself that he will not vanish when unseen. Indeed, Freud recounts in a note that, when left alone, his grandson played the *fort/da* game in front of a mirror by making himself come and go. [14]

In the mirror-house construction of *Watt*, the *fort/da* game, Watt's little game with colors, is repeated on all narrative levels. It is a game invariably played at the border of night and day. Thus, in the omniscient frame, Watt fades from Hackett's view into the evening gloom — "He stood with his back towards them, from the waist up faintly outlined against the last wisps of day." (p. 18) — leaving Hackett in darkness. And at the end of Part IV, in the twilight of morning, after Watt has purchased a ticket to "the further end" of the line (p. 244), the station master, catching sight of what should have been Watt, looks instead "at nothing in particular," the novel's last paragraph repeats twice. Then, within Sam's narrative, Watt fades from Sam's eyes into the shadows, and in Watt's narrative in turn, Mr Knott, compared to the rising and setting sun, is barely glimpsed before returning into the undifferentiated darkness of uncertainty. And finally, again in the evening dusk, Watt sees his hallucinatory double — as unidentifiable and intriguing a figure as he is to others: "Watt was unable to say whether this figure was that of a man, or that of a woman, or that of priest, or that of a nun" (p. 225) — fade in and out of view and finally disappear down the road from the station. There are not several endings as some readers have thought. The various

---

[14] *Beyond the Pleasure Principle*, p. 15, n. 1. The projective and introjective inversions at work in the *fort/da* game will be discussed further in the second part of this study.

fade-outs (Watt from the novel, Watt from Sam's view, the question mark within Watt) chronicle the same unfinished quest within the narrators within narrators, repeat the same game of come and go with elusive traces in the mirror within.

That the echoing voices likewise come and go is most clearly illustrated by the three instances of the voice Watt is quoting. For embedded inside Watt's narrative we find three long digressions, each covering approximately twenty-five pages (like the Hackett segment).[15] Each of the three is heard by Watt after his arrival at Knott's, that is, they are multiple instances of the voice within Watt. The first of these, Arsene's "short statement" (p. 39), which condenses the novel into twenty-four pages, like all the other discourses in the novel is faulty and "entered Watt's ears only by fits" (p. 80). And as Arsene, one of the series of Knott's servants, ends his monologue, he fades from view. In Part II, Watt's tale of a hypothetical series of dogs needed to eat the left-overs of Mr Knott's meal — equally hypothetical — seems inspired by "a particular little voice" of which he could not say whether it was joking or serious (p. 91). And as expected, at the end of twenty-six pages of tedious suppositions, the validity of the statement is denied: "Not that for a moment Watt supposed that he had penetrated the forces at play, in this particular instance..." (p. 117). It is all only a game, a joke played by the "little voice," as is the novel itself. Then, in Part III, Watt listens to Arthur's twenty-six page long story of Mr Louit's report. Although Watt is said to particularly enjoy this account, it, like the others, is inaccurately quoted and fades out without ending. The three digressions mimic the narrative game.

Thus, just like the child's game, the novel's mirror and echo games, the play with images and sounds fading away to blur and murmur, reenact a disconnection. And as in the case of the child, there is no return to a former unity. As witnessed by its horizontal and vertical discontinuities, the text fails to retranscribe the dis-

---

[15] In *Back to Beckett* (Princeton: Princeton Univ. Press, 1973), p. 44, Ruby Cohn points out that the first three parts of *Watt* each contain a long digression from Watt's story. Each digression, she finds, is a narrative within the main narrative.

course heard at different psychical levels or recapture the visual icon of self.

Instead, that the text posits a question is clear not only from the narrative games but also from the narrative structure. The conflicting narrative modes of the previous works are here distributed among what appears at first confusing narrative levels. A non-linear reading, however, has been able to account for the novel's perplexing narrative structure. The narrative levels function like a complex sentence with embeddings inside embeddings, or like a polyphonic score, to use a musical analogy, or like a Chinese box puzzle with each level nested within the other. The latter analogies, however, are not quite adequate, for we must imagine an infinite puzzle, an unending series or *mise en abyme*. [16]

Thus, *Watt*'s interior duplication first splinters a continuous linear narration and then regroups the fragments vertically. Or, in other words, the *mise en abyme* breaks a syntagmatic chain by means of a paradigmatic series. [17] Accordingly, the multiple narrations in *Watt* cannot be aligned horizontally, one next to the other, but vertically: Hackett's echoes Sam's which echoes Watt's which echoes the voices within Watt and so on infinitely. The novel's narrative game strategies thus realign the fragments into a dizzying mirror-house and resonance chamber structure through which the *fort/da* game may be played indefinitely.

The ways Jean Ricardou suggests in which interior duplication energizes what it imitates are easily applied to *Watt*. *Mise en abyme* reenforces by repetition in different terms; secondly, the micro-elements may serve to announce the macro-elements; and thirdly, it provides condensed, schematized replica of the text. [18]

---

[16] Of the three types of *mise en abyme* described by Dällenbach (p. 51), simple, infinite, and paradoxical, it is infinite *mise en abyme* that is at work in *Watt* and the subsequent novels.

For an analysis of nesting or infinite fictions in children's songs and the works of John Barth, Jorge Luis Borges, and others, see the Chapter "Play with Infinity," in Susan Stewart, *Nonsense*, pp. 116-45.

[17] For this view of *mise en abyme*, see Jean Ricardou, *Le Nouveau Roman* (Paris: Seuil, 1973), pp. 73-75. Ricardou illustrates his discussion of abysmal structure with examples from his own works and those of Robbe-Grillet, Butor, Claude Ollier, and Claude Simon. The narrative discontinuity and ingenious games in Beckett's novels long prevented critics from identifying his use of self-reflexive narrative.

[18] *Le Nouveau Roman*, p. 50 f.

In the first instance, Watt's Augustinian discourse parallels Sam's Cartesian version which in turn parallels Hackett's empirical account. The narratives, linked to the archeology of Western thought, receding from empiricism to Cartesianism and beyond to Augustinianism and with Arsene's statement even further to the pre-Socratic tradition are repeated faulty and fragmentary transcriptions of the unknowable, unreachable, unnamable within Watt. (The implication of these orders of discourse will be discussed in the next chapter.) Secondly, Arsene's statement in the first part serves as a prophecy of what is to come in the novel. And thirdly, *Watt* provides a number of emblems of itself: in addition to the mirror game, there are the frequently discussed graphic, musical, mathematical, and linguistic models. Thus, the intriguing picture of dot and circle, broken below, taken by Watt as one of a series, points to the novel's discontinuity, the irreparable disjunction. And in the threne and descant, heard on Watt's way from the station in the first part and to the station in the fourth part respectively, four voices at different ranges — soprano, alto, tenor, and bass — sing fragmentary texts echoing the polyphonic composition of the novel, its transcriptions at different levels.[19] Moreover, the grotesque lists, series, combinations, and permutations that make up a large part of the digressions in Parts II and III, as well as the story of Mr Louit's dissertation on *The Mathematical Intuitions of the Visicelts*, the unfinished manuscript of which was irretrievably lost in the "gentlemen's cloakroom of Ennis railway-station" (p. 173), followed by the Nackybal mathematical hoax, all serve to discredit mathematics as an adequate model of reality. In mathematical terms, they schematize the novel's flawed and suspended state.[20]

---

[19] For further discussions of the painting of the broken circle, see particularly Ruby Cohn, *Samuel Beckett: The Comic Gamut* (New Brunswick, N.J.: Rutgers Univ. Press, 1962), p. 79; Olga Bernal, *Langage et fiction dans le roman de Beckett* (Paris: Gallimard, 1969), pp. 99-102; and Lucien Dällenbach, *Le Récit spéculaire*, pp. 133-37. For other parallels between the musical models and the novel, see Susan Field Senneff, "Song and Music in Samuel Beckett's *Watt*," *Modern Fiction Studies*, 11 (Summer 1964), 137-49.

[20] For this aspect of *Watt*, see John J. Mood, " 'The Personal System' " — Samuel Beckett's *Watt*," *PMLA*, 86 (1971), 255-65; and Hugh Kenner, *Samuel Beckett: A Critical Study* (New York: Grove Press, 1961), pp. 104-05.

The novel's discontinuities are thus mirrored by the inconclusive empiricist, rational, mystic, and cosmological discourses, by pictorial, musical, and mathematical models, and most importantly, by language itself, since for Watt, words have lost their connections to what they refer, so that he could no longer call a pot a pot, or Watt, Watt, or Knott, Knott. The linguistic sign, very much like the little child's toy that is made to disappear and reappear, is a symbolic substitute for the real thing. Since the word is not the thing, the name not the person, language only evokes the thing or the person by substituting for them a sign. Like the child's game, language is a presence, a calling into appearance, of an absence. So that Watt "set to trying names on things, and on himself, almost as a woman hats" (p. 83). In this version of the child's game, the word or name is itself a presence made of absence, a named absence, the absence mastered for a while. [21]

Watt's verbal games further situate language on the border of what Julia Kristeva calls the semiotic and symbolic orders, a border inhabited by all of Beckett's subsequent writing. [22] For Kristeva, it is the function of art and particularly of poetic language and word play to effect a "sémiotisation du symbolique," [23] that is, it is the role of art to infuse into the socio-symbolic order of language the enjoyment *(jouissance)* of the pre-verbal, pre-symbolic play with sound, motion, and color. Although she links the pre-verbal stage to a pre-Oedipal attachment to the mother, it is important to note that Kristeva insists that poetic language or semiotic play does not

---

[21] The formulation of this thought comes from Jacques Lacan, "Fonction et champ de la parole et du langage en psychanalyse" (1956); rpt. in *Ecrits* (Paris: Seuil, 1966), p. 276: "Par le mot qui est déjà une présence faite d'absence, l'absence même vient à se nommer en un moment original dont le génie de Freud a saisi dans le jeu de l'enfant la recréation perpétuelle." / "Through the word — already a presence made of absence — absence itself comes to giving itself a name in that moment of origin whose perpetual recreation Freud's genius detected in the play of the child." The translation is by Anthony Wilden, "The Function of Language in Psychoanalysis," by Jacques Lacan, in *The Language of the Self* (Baltimore: Johns Hopkins Press, 1968), p. 39. For Lacan, language is a *fort/da* game, and the game signals the child's entry into the symbolic order.

[22] See "Sémiotique et Symbolique," in *La Révolution du langage poétique* (Paris: Seuil, 1974), pp. 17-100. See also Kristeva's "Le Père, l'amour, l'exil," in *Cahier Samuel Beckett*, ed. Tom Bishop and Raymond Federman, *L'Herne*, No. 31 (1976), pp. 246-52.

[23] *Révolution du langage poétique*, p. 77.

effect a regression from the socio-symbolic order, but rather injects pre-symbolic *jouissance* into it. It is from this point of view that we can understand the paradoxical Beckettian attack on language through the use of language, the disruption of narrative line through narrative repetition. For the play with sounds, rhythm, forms, syntax, meaning, line, colors, and light constitute a ludic disruption of the symbolic order. *Watt*'s final fragment, "no symbols where none intended," which labels the novel as pre-symbolic play, is to be taken seriously in the manner children are serious at their play.

The startling complexities of *Watt*, the novel's abysmal narrative structure, its unending series of mirror and echo games, which undermine the symbolic order, not only reappear in *Molloy*, written in 1947, but in reduplicated form. In this novel, *Watt*'s narrators and their images in the mirror (a one to one to one and so on *ad infinitum* relationship) become a series of doubles. Beckett's first novel in French, *Mercier et Camier*, written in 1946, begins with the anonymous narrator's description of his relationship to a double persona, "Le voyage de Mercier et Camier, je peux le raconter si je veux, car j'étais avec eux tout le temps." / "The journey of Mercier and Camier is one I can tell, if I will, for I was with them all the time." In *Molloy*, this reduplicated self-reflexivity is developed to the extreme.

Molloy is typographically divided into two parts of roughly equal length, the first, consisting of a brief preamble followed by a single uninterrupted paragraph, narrated by Molloy, the second, composed of a series of paragraphs narrated by Moran. Just as with *Watt*, the puzzling relations between the narrations can be resolved only through a non-linear reading. Whereas the preamble is usually considered Molloy's introduction to his text, a careful reading reveals that the narrator of this opening paragraph can be neither Molloy nor Moran. Chronologically, the preamble follows the two parts; it presents previously written texts to the reader or the "beginning" as the unnamed narrator calls it. The book thus begins at the end (or more accurately, the near-end), and the end at the beginning (the preamble) frames the two first-person narrations it presents.

Who, though, is the narrator of the preamble? Like Molloy and Moran, this narrator speaks in the first person and in the present tense of writing in a room. Like the other two as well, in writing about past and present events, he casts doubt on each statement as soon as it is made. In this manner he mentions his mother like Molloy, his son like Moran, and his writing within the mother's room, Molloy's destination, under the orders of Moran's master(s). It follows that he cannot be identified exclusively with either Molloy or Moran. To the contrary, the relationship among the three narrators is best expressed by the formula: one and one make one.[24] The novel's implicit author, instead of producing a unified text, has splintered it into two by dividing himself into two narrators with opposite points of view.

Is this a repetition of the Hackett-Sam-Watt chain? Yes and no. Yes, in the sense that Hackett's, Sam's, and Watt's narrations are multiple versions of the same elusive discourse, each reflecting the other. Similarly, the parts of *Molloy* mirror each other vertically, but unlike *Watt,* they reflect each other horizontally as well. On the vertical plane, Molloy attempts in vain to transcribe an inner text, "quelque chose de changé dans le silence" (p. 135) / "something gone wrong with the silence" (p. 88). Molloy's partial transcription, however, figures in turn the inner discourse Moran fails to recognize as his own. As such, Molloy's narrative is present in Moran's although unrecognized. And the narrator of the preamble in turn speaks of pages, written by him in the past, marked with signs he can no longer decipher. We have than a text (1) within Molloy, whose text (2) is contained within Moran, whose text (3) is inscribed within the novel's narrator. The three narratives are thus simultaneous versions at different levels of one discourse or the partly decipherable layers of a palimpsest. And as in *Watt,* the three transcriptions are part of unending archives of reverberating texts.

Unlike the multiple narratives of *Watt,* however, *Molloy's* two parts mirror each other horizontally as well. Molloy's and Moran's narratives are antithetical versions of the same story, Molloy and

---

[24] In Jean-Paul Sartre's play, *Les Séquestrés d'Altona* (Paris: Gallimard, 1960), which like *Molloy* echoes many of the themes of the Oedipus story, these words stand out during the concluding soliloquy: "Un et un font un, voilà notre mystère." / "One and one make one — there's our mystery." The English translation, *The Condemned of Altona* (New York: Vintage Books, 1963) is by Sylvia and George Leeson.

Moran mirror images: "Tout le contraire de moi" (p. 175/"Just the opposite of myself" (p. 113) Moran writes of Molloy. The novel's narrator thus sees his reflection broken into two opposing fragments. And then, within each part of *Molloy*, the doubles reduplicate. Just as the unnamed narrator of the preamble is split into two, figuring the schizo-structure of the novel, Molloy in Part I and Moran in Part II narrate in turn their meeting with doubles who then divide before their eyes. The schizo-structure becomes an infinitistic process.

Thus, at the beginning of his narration, or more precisely, self-narration, Molloy (the present narrating self) stages the fading of the senses — "Tout s'estompe.... C'est dans la tête"/"All grows dim.... It's in the head" — announcing the fraying of a path into the psyche: "La route dure et blanche, balafrait les tendres pâturages...."/"The road, hard and white, seared the tender pastures...." Within this psychic space, Molloy (the past narrated self), in the position of elevated observer, sees A and B (A and C in the English version) move toward each other, come face to face, and fade into the evening. In a reduplication of the Hackett-Watt encounter at the beginning of *Watt*, this opening episode stages Molloy watching two parts of himself meet and part. And once again, the psychic fragments do not reform into a totality; they come and they go. Indeed, having stated that he distinguishes himself from A and B only with difficulty — "Il passe des gens aussi, dont il n'est pas facile de se distinguer avec netteté"/"People pass too, hard to distinguish from yourself" — Molloy is tempted to join each of them, a temptation only played out not carried through. Moreover, while identifying with B, he imagines B's contemplating a divided space just as Molloy is doing himself. And since to tell the A/B encounter the narrator slips from the present tense into the past, from "Il passe des gens...."/"People pass..." right into "C'est ainsi que je vis A et B..."/"So I saw A and C...", and since he wavers between the fictional past and present throughout this description, it becomes clear that the reduplication of doubles in the present repeats *ad infinitum* a past inscribed in the psyche.[25]

---

[25] In "Freud et la scène de l'écriture," in *L'Ecriture et la différence*, p. 317, Derrida discusses Freud's comparison of writing with the fraying

The corresponding episode in Part II occurs during the last third of Moran's self-narration. During the three days he is waiting for his son to return with a bicycle (Molloy, as well, speculates that the A/B encounter may have taken place on three days instead of one), Moran, again at dusk, comes face to face with his versions of B (the old man with the club) and A (the dim man). On the first day, Moran, after contemplating his wavering reflection in a stream, meets an old man whose face he desires as his own. On the second day, he sees first an unidentifiable face in the flowing depths of an inner glass and later a man by the campfire whose face, described in terms reminiscent of Moran's likeness in a mirror, resembles Moran's own. And while Moran is looking at this partial reflection of himself (A), it comes apart: "Son corps aussi devenait flou, comme s'il se disjoignait" (p. 234). "His body too grew dim, as if coming asunder" (p. 151). Three reflections of one, Moran and his refracted images, disjointed in turn, repeat the A/B episode in part one and the novel's structure.

The anonymous narrator (x) sees himself within the mirror as Molloy and Moran facing each other as specular doubles. Each of the doubles sees the other (within this mirror within a mirror) not as one but split into A and B, who in turn see double, and so on infinitely. Or, in mathematical terms, the narrative structure of *Molloy* is analogous to continued fractions:

---

of a path and links this metaphor to the deferred production of meaning in the present, of events inscribed in the past: "La métaphore du chemin frayé, si fréquente dans les descriptions de Freud, communique toujours avec le thème du *retardement supplémentaire* et de la reconstitution du sens après-coup.... Le post-scriptum qui constitue le présent passé comme tel ne se contente pas, comme l'ont peut-être pensé Platon, Hegel et Proust, de le réveiller ou de le révéler dans sa vérité. Il le produit." The English translation by Mehlman, in *Yale French Studies*, p. 96, reads as follows: "The metaphor of the frayed path, so frequent in Freud's descriptions, is always in communication with the theme of the *supplementary delay* and the reconstitution of meaning through deferment.... The postscript which constitutes the past present as such is not satisfied, as Plato, Hegel, and Proust perhaps thought, with reawakening or revealing it in its truth. It produces it."

$$\times$$

Molloy	$+$	Moran
$\overline{A+B}$		$\overline{A+B}$
$\overline{C+D}$		$\overline{C+D}$
$\overline{F+G}$		$\overline{F+G}$

and
so
on

The open-ended narrative structure thus repeats the failure of the series of narrators/protagonists to come face to face with other than endlessly refracted images.

As infinitistic process, then, *Molloy* redoubles *Watt*'s infinite regression. In *Watt*, x (the anonymous narrator) = a (Hackett) = b (Sam) = c (Watt) = d (Arsene) = ?, whereas in *Molloy*, as we have seen, x = Molloy + Moran = (a + b) + (a + b), and so on. And like *Watt*, *Molloy* contains condensed models of its intricate structure. On the one hand, Moran's description of the symbolic language of the bees points to the novel's vertical symmetries. A bee dances at several heights — three or four Moran specifies — but performs intricate variations in hum and figure on the various levels (pp. 261-62/pp. 168-69). On the other hand, the knife-rest, that intrigues Molloy and with which Moran toys, consists of two X's — two intersected lines (twice) with multiple symmetrical features — joined by a mediating term, that is, the two unknowables on each end of the narrative chain. Moreover, at the end of his puzzled contemplation of the knife-rest, Molloy concludes with the famous passage about the soothing knowledge of the unknowable, "savoir ne rien pouvoir savoir, voilà par où passe la paix..." (p. 96)/"to know you are beyond knowing anything, that is when peace enters in..." (p. 64) and by a reference immediately following to the "true division" of twenty-two by seven, that is, of pi, which like the irrational numbers in *Watt* and the continued fractions goes on endlessly.[26]

Certain pronouncements in the earlier novel *Mercier et Camier* also announce the vertical and horizontal open-endedness of

---

[26] For the role of irrational numbers in Beckett's works, see Hugh Kenner, *Samuel Beckett: A Critical Study*, pp. 104-14.

Molloy. At one point, one of the double persona remarks: "C'est drôle, dit Mercier, j'ai souvent l'impression que nous ne sommes pas seuls.... Comme la présence d'un tiers, dit Mercier. Elle nous enveloppe" (p. 170)./"Strange impression, said Mercier, strange impression sometimes that we are not alone.... Like the presence of a third party, said Mercier. Enveloping us" (p. 100). At another point, the twosome becomes a couple of open-ended texts: "Même ensemble, dit Mercier ... il se passe à chaque instant plus de choses que n'en pourrait contenir un gros livre, deux gros livres, le tien et le mien" (p. 145)./"Even side by side, said Mercier ... we are fraught with more events than could fit in a fat tome, two fat tomes, your fat tome and my fat tome" (p. 87).

It is striking that in the art criticism he wrote shortly after *Molloy*, Beckett concentrates on the representational crisis in modern painting in terms evocative of the process of infinite regression staged in his novels of the forties. In "Peintres de l'empêchement" (1948), one of several essays on the same subject, Beckett first restates the Kantian dilemma of the unknowable object: "Car que reste-t-il de représentable si l'essence de l'objet est de se dérober à la représentation?"/"For what remains of the representable if the essence of the object is to elude representation?"[27] The writer then goes on to describe Geer and Bram van Velde's art in terms of the interior duplication of an impenetrable space, variously likened to entombment and incarceration, or in terms of a series of semi-transparencies, one behind the other, an endless montage of partly transparent planes, leading in the direction of the representation of the unrepresentable:

> Est peint ce qui empêche de peindre.... Un dévoilement sans fin, voile derrière voile, plan sur plan de transparences imparfaites, un dévoilement vers l'indévoilable, le rien, la chose à nouveau. Et l'ensevelissement dans l'unique, dans un lieu d'impénétrables proximités, cellule peinte sur la pierre de la cellule, art d'incarcération.
>
> Painted is that which makes painting impossible.... An unveiling without end, veil behind veil, superimposed planes of imperfect transparencies, an unveiling in the

---

[27] "Peintres de l'empêchement," *Derrière le Miroir*, Nos. 11 and 12 (June 1948), p. 4. (My translation.)

direction of what cannot be unveiled, nothingness, the thing anew. And the entombment in uniqueness, in a place of impenetrable proximities, a cell painted on the stone of a cell, an art of incarceration. [28]

It is the opaqueness of the object to the perceiving eye or "I," that generates the painting's or the text's endless self-reflexivity. [29]

In the paintings of the Van Veldes then, Beckett recognized the *mise en abyme* he inscribed so well in his own novels of the forties. His reference to an art of incarceration, however, brings to mind a more distant pictorial example of endless reduplication, Piranesi's famous *Carceri*. Like Bram van Velde's paintings and Beckett's novels, Piranesi's engravings of imaginary prisons repeat themselves within themselves and from one to the other. And as the artist's productions becomes self-producing, he is imprisoned in his own labyrinthic constructions. [30] How well this art of incarceration applies to Beckett will become more and more obvious.

In light of the unknowable, the unrepresentable, Beckett's novels from *Watt* onward, staging but a few moments along the infinite chain, teasingly manipulate and undermine the classic project of the novel to mirror outer and inner reality, the fiction of transparency. The disarticulation of fictional discourse and of language itself, that *Watt* pursues, is replayed in *Molloy* on the narrative, thematic, and textual levels. Thus, the infinite narrative

---

[28] "Peintres de l'empêchement," p. 7. (My translation.) It is interesting to compare this passage on the Van Veldes with the following description by the narrator of *L'Innommable*, written a year later: "L'air, l'air, essayons voir ce qu'il y a à tirer de ce vieux thème. D'un gris tout juste transparent dans mon voisinage immédiat, en dehors de ce cercle charmé il s'étale en fines nappes impénétrables, d'un ton à peine plus foncé" (p. 26). / "Air, the air, is there anything to be squeezed from that old chestnut? Close to me it is grey, dimly transparent, and beyond that charmed circle deepens and spreads its fine impenetrable veils" (p. 300).

[29] In the chapter entitled "Le Dilemme de la représentation," in *Langage et fiction*, p. 126, Olga Bernal writes: "L'invalidité du rapport entre celui qui représente et ce qui est représenté condamne le discours au reflet indéfini de lui-même." / "The invalidity of the relation between the one who represents and what is represented condemns discourse to the indefinite reflection of itself." (My translation.)

[30] In "Abysmal Influence: Baudelaire, Coleridge, De Quincey, Piranesi, Wordsworth," *Glyph*, 4 (1978), 193, Arden Reed specifies: "It is this self-duplicating power that imprisons the artist: his creations become self-creating and swallow him up."

mirror game in *Molloy* is thematically linked to the categories of the central psychoanalytic myth. The game is the same as in *Watt*, only the pieces differ. To give in to the temptation of chess terminology, the preamble's narrator sees himself aligned as queen and king: is he his mother (the son who has taken his mother's place — Molloy)? is he his father (the father who has lost his son — Moran)? True to the *fort/da* game, Molloy and Moran try their mother/father identifications on and off. (More on this in the next chapter.) In turn, their self-narrations of past journeys, the first under the sign of the mother, the second of the father, are only forms of hide and seek: Molloy's narrative is but a faulty translation of interrupted silence (p. 135/p. 88), Moran's a game of come and go. After having written a story, called meaning into the presence of a text, Moran makes it disappear with his final words: "Alors je rentrai dans la maison et j'écrivis, Il est minuit, La pluie fouette les vitres. Il n'était pas minuit. Il ne pleuvait pas." /"Then I went back into the house and wrote, It is midnight. The rain is beating on the windows. It was not midnight. It was not raining." Moran's metanarrative statement effectively says: I was just playing, making statements appear and disappear, to pass the time. I have written about nothing.

All novels, of course, are framed by a number of metacommunicative statements, both direct and indirect, which affect how the novel is read. The outermost frame consists of the cover and copyright pages which mark the text off as a commercial product, as a marketable book. (The price, the cover layout, the book format, the name of the publisher, the time and place of publication, all play a role in the way readers will approach the text.) The next frame may be called the authorial frame which indicates that the novel is the work of a particular writer and follows certain genre conventions, i.e., a novel by Samuel Beckett. This frame consequently labels the work a fiction. (The identity and reputation of the writer, the date and place of writing, and genre expectations, all play a role on this level.) Then, still further on, with the fictional voice of the narrator, a narrative frame is set. The narrator claims that a true story is being told (more or less reliably) and anchors the narrative — and possibly, the narrating act — in person, time, and place. (The latter convention is particularly evident in certain eighteenth century novels in which an additional narrative voice was interposed between the authorial and narrative frames to insure the authenticity of the tale.) In general, then, novels are circumscribed by the following three frames with their corresponding metacommunicative labels:

>The publisher's frame: This is a commodity.
>The authorial frame: This is fiction.
>The narrative frame: This is a true story.

The authorial and narrative frames set up a paradoxical situation that can, however, be resolved: since the authorial frame is of a higher logical type, its metacommunicative label holds. In this way, in ordinary discourse, the metacomunicative comment or nonverbal signal implying, "I was only kidding," can shift the meaning of a statement from insult to play, from negative to positive, and vice versa. That is, "I hate you" is to be understood "I love you" given the appropriate metacommunicative signals. The latter determine the meaning of the statement.[31] Similarly, the authorial frame labels the narrative a fiction despite the narrator's contentions to the contrary, a convention well understood by readers.

What happens in *Molloy*, though? Here again, Beckett deviates from the expected. Instead of contradicting the authorial frame by insisting on authenticity, the narrative voices mimic the authorial label by pointing to the fictional mode of their discourse:

>authorial frame: This is fiction.
>narrative frame (the preamble's narrator): Everything is uncertain about my story.
>narrative frame (Molloy): This story is a lie.
>narrative frame (Moran): This story is a lie.

---

[31] Gregory Bateson, et al. — "Toward a Theory of Schizophrenia" (1956); rpt. in *Ecology of Mind*, pp. 201-27 — analyzing metacommunicative labels with the help of Bertrand Russell's Theory of Logical Types, write on p. 203: "Even among the lower mammals there appears to be an exchange of signals which identify certain meaningful behavior as 'play,' etc. These signals are evidently of higher Logical Type than the messages they classify. Among human beings this framing and labeling of messages and meaningful actions reaches considerable complexity...."

Contrary to the conventions of the novel, the narrative frames insist on the fictional modality or on writing as play. Indeed, the narrator Molloy's metanarrative statement, "je ne fais que me plier aux exigences d'une convention qui veut qu'on mente ou qu'on se taise" (p. 135)/"I am merely complying with the convention that demands you either lie or hold your peace" (p. 88), reiterates the point of view that all language is but a fictionalization of unnamable processes, a trying on and off of meaning. What his words describe is what did not take place.[32]

Besides their metacommunicative disclaimers, both Molloy and Moran disassociate themselves from their self-narrations in still another way when they abandon the first person to refer to themselves in the third person at the end of their texts. The first part concludes with the following statement: "Molloy pouvait rester, là où il était."/"Molloy could stay, where he happened to be." About the voice he hears, Moran writes just before the final dismantling statement: "Elle ne se servait pas des mots qu'on avait appris au petit Moran, que lui à son tour avait appris à son petit."/"It did not use the words that Moran had been taught when he was little and that he in his turn had taught to his little one." Narrator and narrated fail to coincide; the first person was only another cover to try on and off.

The many other ways in which the narrators of *Molloy* poke holes into the fabric of their texts have been amply documented.

---

[32] For another reading of Beckett's self-cancelling fictions, see Raymond Federman, "Samuel Beckett: The Liar's Paradox," in *Samuel Beckett: The Art of Rhetoric*, ed. Edouard Morot-Sir, et al. (Chapel Hill: North Carolina Studies in the Romance Languages and Literatures, 1976), pp. 119-41. Federman (p. 131) points out that Beckett's fictions from *Molloy* onward denounce the illusory aspect of fiction by passing from "a language that tells *a* story to a language that tells *its* own story," thus effecting a shift from one level of rhetoric to another. Similarly, in *Structure de la Trilogie*, p. 88, Dina Sherzer, after referring to Bateson's notion of framing, finds that the metacommunicative statements in the Three Novels point to the stories and narrations as writing: "Tous les énoncés du méta-récit et ceux de la méta-narration constituent des *cadres* dans lesquels le narrateur dit explicitement 'j'écris.' " / "All the statements of the metafiction and of the metanarration constitute frames within which the narrator explicitly states 'I am writing.' " (My translation.) From our analysis it follows that *Watt*'s and *Molloy*'s disarticulations do not only point to the self-reflexive writing process or to fiction as language, but more drastically turn fiction, writing, and language, together with all systems of meaning, into abysmal play.

Among the more systematic, Dina Sherzer's semiotic study discusses the Three Novels' "rhétorique du discrédit."[33] Among the rhetoric devices that serve to discredit the text, Sherzer lists the metatextual interventions which, like so many glosses on the novel, sabotage both the reports as they are being written and the act of writing itself. Thus, throughout both parts of *Molloy*, the narratives are punctuated with the type of uncertainty Molloy expresses about the A/B incident, "Et je confonds peut-être plusieurs occasions différentes, et les heures..." (p. 19)/"And I am perhaps confusing several different occasions, and different times..." (p. 14), and "Je me demande ce que ça veut dire" (p. 20)./"I wonder what that means" (p. 15). In addition to these, the horizontal continuity of the plots is perturbed by other interruptions that shift the attention from the story-line to the narrator, i.e., allusions to the present state of the narrator, appeals to an implicit reader, the intrusion of opinions, personal exclamations, and atemporal generalizations like, "A l'homo mensura il faut du staffage" (p. 95)/"Homo mensura can't do without staffage" (p. 63), and finally different forms of word play. According to Sherzer, the narrators' play with sounds, forms, meanings (puns, cliché deformations, semantic violations), syntactic categories (especially verb tenses), style registers, as well as the frequent allusions to other texts, all function to render the narrative opaque, to draw attention to the writing itself. From our previous analysis, it follows that the ultimate status of language is that of a toy, a symbolic subsitute for what remains absent, a toy the narrators manipulate with increasing dexterity.

On the novel's textual surface, it is perhaps the struggle with verb tenses that most insistently mocks language as representation. When one examines the different temporalities of *Molloy*, one notices that a present discourse frames the double self-narrative of the anonymous narrator: "Oui, *je travaille* maintenant..." (p. 7)/"Yes, *I work* now..." (p. 7), and each of the two parts, Molloy's, "Cette fois-ci, puis encore une *je pense*..." (p. 9)/"This time, then once more *I think*..." (p. 8), and Moran's, *"Je me*

---

[33] *Structure de la Trilogie*, p. 86. Sherzer in turn borrowed the phrase from Bernard Pingaud, "'Dire, c'est inventer,'" *Quinzaine Littéraire*, No. 67 (Feb. 1969), p. 5.

rappelle le jour où je reçus l'ordre de m'occuper de Molloy" (p. 142)./ "*I remember* they day I received the order to see about Molloy" (p. 92). (Emphasis added) Then, within each part, the present tense, calling attention to a narrator writing in a room, interrupts the self-narrative chronicled in the literary past tense reserved for representative writing. As it were, the present of the narrating self runs parallel to the past of the narrated self in order to point to the fictional play of writing and the fictional play with events. In addition, however, the present contests the past tense. Molloy tends to slip from the fictional past into the narrative present or the "mythological present" which he defines as speaking in the present tense when speaking of the past (p. 37/p. 26). But then Molloy, as we know, is not speaking of the past as such but of vague tracings within his psyche whose relation to the past is problematical. Mythic time, the present endlessly repeating the past, is the proper temporality of this elusive psychic material, the text within Molloy.

The following passage at the beginning of Molloy's narrative (pp. 9-10/pp. 8-9) illustrates the oscillation between the past tense and the two forms of the present:

> C'*était* sur une route d'une nudité frappante, je *veux dire* sans haies ... car dans d'immenses champs des vaches *mâchaient*.... J'*invente* peut-être un peu, j'*embellis* peut-être, mais dans l'ensemble c'*était* ainsi. Elles *mâchent,* puis *avalent,* puis après une courte pause *appellent* sans effort la prochaine bouchée.... Mais c'*est* peut-être là des souvenirs.

> It *was* on a road remarkably bare, I *mean* without hedges ... for cows *were chewing* in enormous fields.... Perhaps *I'm* inventing a little, perhaps embellishing, but on the whole that's the way it *was.* They *chew, swallow,* then after a short pause effortlessly *bring* up the next mouthful.... But perhaps *I'm remembering* things. (Emphasis added)

The present tense, on the one hand, refers to the motion of pen on paper within a room; the fictional past to motion through fields, towns, gardens, forests; the mythological present to retracing processes of the mind, perhaps inventions, perhaps memories. The chronological and linear progression of events in the past, however, is contested not only by the present tenses, but perturbed by irregular plotting, by flashbacks, by multiple embeddings from a more or less distant past, a time whose infinite layers no tense can accurately describe.[34] An infinite series of pluperfects would be required. For finally, there are no verb tenses as there are no words that adequately translate the little disturbances of silence with which Molloy plays his narrative game of come and go: "Ma vie, ma vie, tantôt j'en parle comme d'une chose finie, tantôt comme d'une plaisanterie qui dure encore, et j'ai tort, car elle est finie et elle dure à la fois, mais par quel temps du verbe exprimer cela?" (p. 53)./"My life, my life, now I speak of it as of something over, now as of a joke which still goes on, and it is neither, for at the same time it is over and it goes on, and is there any tense for that?" (p. 36).

After *Molloy*, the intricate narrative games are renewed, increasingly well played out, but basically the same. The horizontal discontinuities found in *Molloy*, the metanarrative strategies that serve to rupture the textual surface, undermine in similar fashion the texts of the subsequent novels.[35] And on the vertical plane, the narrators of succeeding texts — one fitting into the other in an infinite narrative puzzle — replay versions of the same game. Thus, to recapitulate:

The Metanarrative Fort/Da *Game*

The game of come and go with unknowable inner traces frames each narrative. It turns each text into play. In *Malone meurt/Malone Dies*, written in 1948, a few months after *Molloy*, a narrator for the first time expressly tags his writing with the metacommunicative label of "play": "C'est un jeu maintenant, je vais jouer" (p. 9)./"Now it is a game, I am going to play" (p. 180). Thus, Malone recalls his chiaroscuro diversions with fictional fragments:

---

[34] Sherzer (p. 31 ff.) analyzes the embedded flashbacks under the category of an anterior past narrative, a "récit-passé antérieur."

[35] In addition to Sherzer, see Brian T. Fitch, *Dimensions, structures et textualité dans la trilogie romanesque de Beckett* (Paris: Minard, 1977). Since this aspect of the novels has been amply discussed, I will not repeat the arguments for each novel.

"J'allumais partout, je regardais bien autour de moi, je me mettais à jouer avec ce que je voyais.... Mais je ne tardais pas à me retrouver seul, sans lumière" (pp. 9-10)./"I turned on all the lights, I took a good look all around, I began to play with what I saw.... But it was not long before I found myself alone, in the dark" (p. 180). And after resolving to play, that is, to fictionalize, as much as possible from now on, he considers the possibility of finding himself again abandoned in the dark: "Alors je jouerai tout seul, je ferai comme si je me voyais" (p. 10), reads the French text, which Beckett himself translated into, "Then I shall play with myself" (p. 180), whereas a literal translation would read, "Then I shall play all by myself, pretending I can see myself." Where Beckett's 1954-56 translation implies autoerotic play, the original French version — like the novel's first title "L'Absent" — strongly suggests the abandoned child's game with his image in the mirror and the earlier fictional series of self-reflexive games.[36]

Malone plays three different ways: he writes stories about yet another persona in the past which, like previous fictions, make the narrator's own image emerge uncertainly and vanish; he describes his present state which oscillates between imminent birth and death, presence and absence; and thirdly, he makes an inventory of his possessions that shows the narrator's symbolic toys appearing and disappearing. Three versions of hide and seek, of *fort/da*, the games first alternate, then merge into one. As his possessions disappear, Malone nears death, his stories end, until within the strategy of come and go, all sink back into the unknowable dark until the next round of play.

The narrator of *L'Innommable/The Unnamable,* written a year after *Malone meurt,* calls back the inner reflections from Murphy through Malone and sends them off again. Quite clearly, as the latest narrator of the series, he refers to them as fragments broken off from himself which he had hoped to inspect (p. 33/pp. 303-04). Then, despite the doubts he expresses about the game, the Unnamable, in a paroxysm of play, invents and extinguishes another set of opposing fictions, repeatedly calls himself the only one present, the only one absent, disconnects, reconnects, disconnects

---

[36] Ruby Cohn indicates the original title of *Malone meurt* in *Back to Beckett*, p. 92.

parts of the body, parts of speech, counts all language a game of come and go.

Written in the early fifties, the *Textes pour rien/Texts for Nothing* read like more of *L'Innommable:* "Et je suis encore en route, par oui et par non, vers un encore à nommer..." (p. 203)./ "And it's still the same old road I'm trudging, up yes and down no, towards one yet to be named..." (p. 127). The unnamed narrator of the thirteen texts repeats the peekaboo with the unknowable: "coucou me voilà... comme la racine carrée de moins un..." (p. 205)./"But peekaboo here I come again... like the square root of minus one..." (p. 128). Each text is a game of come and go, each rising from nothing, swelling out into a gamut of contradictory possibilities, then subsiding back into nothing. Each time it is a silence that can be broken by the next text.

Finally, *Comment c'est/How It Is,* written in 1959-60, and the subsequent short prose pieces play on. *Comment c'est*'s fragments of syntax, like *Watt*'s tattered text, record only snatches from a fading voice. Brief scenes from a life up in the light flicker on and off in the dark. And Malone's three forms of play, description, fiction, possessions, instead of pulsating alternatively, intermingle. And as in *Molloy,* the end labels the narrative a lie: "de la foutaise d'un bout à l'autre" (p. 174)/"all balls from start to finish" (p. 144). As well, the later short pieces (and plays), *Play,* for example, and *Bing/Ping,* composed in the early and mid-sixties, and *Pour finir encore/For to End Yet Again,* dating from the mid-seventies, stage an inner space where sounds fade away and vague apparitions shade in and out of black, or white, or gray.

Vertical and Horizontal Reduplication

Like *Watt* and *Molloy,* the subsequent novels inscribe an infinite series of self-duplicating narrators, the writer's version of the multiplication of the self within the self. And from *Watt* onward, as we have seen, the stratified structure is repeated not only within each text, but from one to the other. As we read from earlier texts to the later, we find each one contained within the other, Molloy's narration within Moran's within Malone's within the Unnamable's. Each new narration, attempting a translation of the elusive inner text, forms another link in the infinite chain, neither going back to origin nor attaining end.

Malone meurt playfully stages this proliferation of embedded narrators. Because of his allusion to the circumstances and vague reminiscences of the unnamed narrator of *Molloy*'s preamble, Malone may be identified with this writer, giving the chain Molloy-Moran-Malone. This sequence is continued in one direction by Malone's supposition that he is in a head, but not his own (p. 87/ p. 221). In this sense, Malone is himself another interior duplication. In the other direction, the series recedes from Molloy to Mercier, Watt, and Murphy, mentioned as doubles by Malone and Moran. (In *Mercier et Camier,* in turn, Watt reappears and Murphy is mentioned.)

In addition, Malone produces another self-portrait, the doubly named Sapo-Macmann, whose story, surprisingly enough, is told in the third person. Unlike the superimposed first-person narrations of *Molloy, Malone meurt* embeds a third-person narrative within a first-person discourse, as is true of the Sam-Watt narrations. Like *Watt,* too, *Malone meurt* provides a number of metaphors for its labyrinthic inner space, so that we find Sapo-Macmann in the psyche of Malone (landscape or asylum) who in turn is in the head or womb of a yet unnamed narrator (the room). (*Fin de partie/Endgame* stages a similar reduplication of inner space: the gray shelter-like room of the mind with two high windows as eyes contains the blind and crippled Hamm playing at creating stories in his mind.)

The last section of *Malone meurt* features a metanarrative spoof of the Beckettian chain of doubles, a type of extended self-parody. In Malone's fiction, Lemuel (a form of Samuel, as often pointed out) is in charge of the inner asylum's patients. In addition to Macmann, Lemuel rounds up four other asylum inmates for an excursion. The four, two English, two French speakers, caricature Murphy — "un homme jeune, mort jeune, assis dans un vieux rocking-chair" (p. 204)/"a young man, dead young, seated in an old rocking-chair" (p. 281) — then Watt — "What! s'exclama-t-il" (p. 206)/"What! he exclaimed" (p. 282) (Without quotes in the text) — and more vaguely, either Moran and Molloy or Mercier and Camier. The inmates set off tied two by two, paired off as opposites. Then, with an intertextual wink in the direction of *Six Characters in Search of an Author,* at nightfall — the necessary twilight setting for the chiaroscuro diversions — the six characters move out to sea. All merge into one as they fade into the night: "Ils ne sont plus, dans la nuit, qu'un seul amas, silencieux, visibles à peine..." (p. 216)./"Silent, dim... they lie together in a heap, in the night" (p. 287). The story mirroring Malone's self-narration thus in turn contains an abyss, a playful repetition of earlier interior duplications.

Horizontally, *Malone meurt,* unlike *Molloy* and many of the other novels, is not divided into three or four parts, but into many paragraphs of varying lengths. Malone's modes of self-reflexive narration — he writes about fictional fragments of himself in the guise of first-person reflections and third-person reduplications, that is, the characters and objects that possess him, all of which he encases in the metanarrative game — alternate discontinuously throughout the novel until they merge into one at the end. Surprisingly, Malone's first-person discourse has been described as direct self-quotation or as an interior monologue giving no indication of how it came to be written down.[37] Malone, to the contrary, insists that he is playing, using various narrative strategies to make fragments of the self come and go, playing with writing. Consequently, Malone's activity as a writer is foregrounded by such parodic comments as: "Je viens d'écrire. Je crois que j'ai encore dormi, etc. J'espère que je ne dénature pas trop ma pensée"

---

[37] Genette — "Discours du récit," p. 240 / *Narrative Discourse,* p. 230 — writes: "rien ne prétend que Meursault ou Malone aient écrit le texte que nous lisons comme leur monologue intérieur.... c'est le propre du discours immédiat que d'exclure toute détermination de forme de l'instance narrative qu'il constitue." / "nothing claims that Meursault or The Unnamable wrote the texts we read as their interior monologues.... It is the nature of immediate speech to preclude any formal determination of the narrating instance which it constitutes." It is interesting to speculate how the "Malone" of Genette's original French became "The Unnamable" in the English translation. Could it be that someone pointed out the error about Malone's mode? However, since the Unnamable also fabricates a fiction about his writing, although he cannot lift his hand from his knee (p. 28 / p. 301), and comments frequently on the paradoxical situation of being narrated by the fictions he is narrating, his metanarrative spoofs of narrating and writing conventions place his discourse on the opposite pole from immediate thought quotation or self-quoted interior monologue.

(p. 63) / "I have just written, I fear I must have fallen, etc. I hope this is not too great a distortion of the truth" (p. 208).

In *L'Innommable,* wheels within wheels proliferate. In the preamble, the novel's first-person narrator tells of Malone revolving around him and imagines present the entire narrative series, in which he includes himself: "A vrai dire, je les crois tous ici, à partir de Murphy tout au moins, je nous crois tous ici..." (p. 11). / "To tell the truth I believe they are all here, at least from Murphy on, I believe we are all here..." (p. 293). Or he mockingly locates them and himself in pit under pit under pit: "Y a-t-il d'autres fonds, plus bas? Auxquels on accède par celui-ci? Stupide hantise de la profondeur" (p. 11). / "Are there other pits, deeper down? To which one accedes by mine? Stupid obsession with depth" (p. 293). Finally, though, the preamble substitutes for the vertical abyss a different representation of infinity, an asymptotic relation between the Unnamable and the doubles that orbit about him. Although the word "asymptote" (Greek *a-*, not, and *sumptōtos*, from *sumpiptein*, to fall together) is not mentioned directly, the text in several places hints at its etymology by staging the "falling together" of two revolving figures. The Unnamable describes, for instance, two shapes whose curved paths meet "symptotically" instead of asymptotically near him. They collide, fall, and disappear (p. 19) / pp. 296-97), a path the narrator would prefer the other reduplications to follow.

After the preamble, in an uninterrupted paragraph of 230 pages (in the French edition), the Unnamable, imagining himself repeatedly in a head, embeds multiple versions of the unending series of narrators in his discourse:

The endless chain of voices

> Ils sont nombreux, tout autour, se tenant la main peut-être, chaîne sans fin, se tenant les chaînons, parlant à tour de rôle. (p. 141) / They are numerous, all round, holding hands perhaps, an endless chain, taking turns to talk. (p. 356)

The proliferation of clichés

In another replay of past self-portraits — "cette fois c'est le grand jeu" (p. 183) / "this may mean something" (p. 377) — others attempt to force an identity upon the Unnamable by means of photographs and files upon photographs and files, parodying the Murphy, Watt, Molloy, Malone sequence.

The series of anonymities

Soon after the rejection of former cliché reproductions of self, the Unnamable imagines one, then two, then three unknowables like himself becoming a "rêve sans fin" (p. 187) / "perpetual dream" (p. 378) and compares the multitude to the famous round song featured in *Godot,* an example of double textual reduplication, since the verses of the song repeat themselves, as pointed out by the narrator, the third verse doubling the first, the fourth the second, the fifth the third, and so on, *ad infinitum,* and within the song, the written tale of the dog's death and burial is endlessly replicated. (The two verses that double and redouble themselves within the song suggest a similar reduplication for *Godot*'s two acts. The acts of this two-act play are two of an infinite series.)

The generations of caged beasts

The words that speak through the Unnamable tell him he is like a "bête née en cage de bêtes nées en cage de bêtes nées en cage..." (p. 204) / "a caged beast born of caged beasts born of caged beasts..." (p. 386) looking for such a beast.

Repetition as play

Finally, the eleven-page sentence (French edition, pp. 200-11), illustrating the theoretically infinite recursive patterns of a sentence, repeats, before and after the caged beasts sequence embedded within it, a string of losts and founds, hide and seek:

> ...trouvant pourquoi, ne trouvant plus, retrouvant, ne retrouvant plus, ne cherchant plus, cherchant encore, trouvant encore, ne trouvant plus, ne cherchant plus, cherchant encore, ne trouvant rien, trouvant enfin, ne trouvant plus... perdant la boule, cherchant la boule... (p. 201)
>
> ...finding the cause, losing it again, finding it again, not finding it again, seeking no longer, seeking again, finding again, losing again, finding nothing, finding at last, losing

again... [The French pun on losing and seeking one's marbles is omitted in the English version.] (p. 385)

As in previous novels, the infinite series is the expansion of a threesome. The Unnamable produces Mahood, another mirror image — "nous voilà face à face, Mahood et moi, si nous sommes deux..." (p. 57) / "there we are face to face, Mahood and I, if we are twain..." (p. 315) — and the "anti-Mahood" Worm. The narrator emphasizes that it is not he who is narrating Mahood's stories; it is Mahood who is narrating his own story while trying to convince the Unnamable it is his doing. Similar to *Molloy*'s narrative posture, the two Mahood stories that follow are retrospective self-narrations, shifting back and forth from past to present, embedded in a first-person discourse. In *L'Innommable*, however, the first-person narrator (the Unnamable) punctuates his text with reminders that it is a third person (Mahood) speaking through his first-person. Since the stories are by Mahood about Mahood using the Unnamable's first person to convince him he is Mahood, they are pseudo-self-narrations, another lie (p. 86 / p. 329) in which the latest narrator finds himself imprisoned.[38]

When speaking of Worm, who unlike Mahood cannot speak, it is a number of voices speaking through the Unnamable: "...Worm, c'est une idée qu'ils ont, un mot qu'ils ont, en parlant d'eux..." (p. 163) / "...Worm, he's an idea they have, a word they use, when speaking of them..." (p. 366). Thus, to speak of Worm, the Unnamable switches to the third person and uses present or future tenses. For a time, then, the third-person attempts at description (Worm cannot be spoken of except negatively) are surrounded by a first-person discourse until the Unnamable temporarily abandons even this first person for the third, "Je ne dirai plus moi.... Je mettrai à la place... la troisième personne, si j'y pense" (p. 139). / "I shall not say I again.... I shall put in its place... the third person, if I think of it" (p. 355). It does not matter, however, whether the narrator uses the first person to claim that it is the

---

[38] The text gives repeated metanarrative indications that, "C'est toujours Mahood qui parle" (p. 68) / "Still Mahood speaking" (p. 320), or "je cite Mahood" (p. 66) "I quote Malone" (p. 320). The substitution of Malone for Mahood is most likely a printing error.

third, or the third person as replacement for the first, juggles with superimposed narrations, first-person on first-person, first-person on third on first, or any of the other combinations tried, since as is true of verb tenses, no pronoun, no narrative voice can reproduce the unnamable forces within.

Since no names or pronouns can speak the Unnamable, no words or murmurs "l'impensable indicible" (p. 98) / "the unthinkable unspeakable" (p. 335), the text's excessively long paragraph and sentences figure, on the syntagmatic axis, the infinite recursiveness of language or a labyrinthic prison of words. To gnaw at this prison, *L'Innommable* undermines words by its textual play with the shifting ground of language. The novel's well-known orienting questions, "Où maintenant? Quand maintenant? Qui maintenant?" / "Where now? Who now? When now?" give rise not to answers but to playful manipulations of names, pronouns, verb tenses, and of the other deictic forms or shifters ("now," "then," "here," "there," and so on) that usually serve to anchor the speaker / narrator in time and space.[39] The narrator, however, suffers from the recognition that language fails to serve as an instrument of self-representation, suffers this condition as if it were an exile, and — like the abandoned child — plays the games reluctantly. In his inaugural lecture at the Collège de France, on 7 January 1977, Roland Barthes, on the other hand, points out that what determines the very status of literature or writing is such a displacement of language, the contesting of language from inside language, the devious play with words. From this point of view, *L'Innommable* is not an extreme example of anti-literature but a *mise en scène* of what is at work in writing.[40]

---

[39] At the beginning of the chapter "Deixis, Space, and Time," in *Semantics* (Cambridge: Cambridge Univ. Press, 1977), II, 636-724, John Lyons defines deixis in the following way: "The term 'deixis' (which comes from a Greek word meaning 'pointing' or 'indicating') is now used in linguistics to refer to the function of personal and demonstrative pronouns, of tense and of a variety of other grammatical and lexical features which relate utterances to the spatio-temporal co-ordinates of the act of utterance."

See also Roman Jakobson, "Shifters, Verbal Categories, and the Russian Verb" (1957); rpt. in *Selected Writings*, II (The Hague: Mouton, 1971), 130-47.

[40] See *Leçon* (Paris: Seuil, 1978), pp. 16-17: "J'entends par *littérature*... la pratique d'écrire. Je vise donc en elle, essentiellement, le texte,

Again, on the paradigmatic axis, since no fictions can truly reflect the "inimaginable" (p. 259) / "unimaginable" (p. 413), the infinite self-reflexivity of the narrative chain confines the narrator, in the manner of Piranesian prisons or the art of incarceration Beckett saw in Bram van Velde's painting, within the endless self-reproducing discourse of his own productions, an abyss of lies.[41] It is the line of pseudo-self-portraits — Mahood, Malone, Moran, Molloy, Mercier, Watt, Murphy, and so on — that tried to tell the Unnamable who he (?) is by means of "cet enfer d'histoires" (p. 190) / "this hell of stories" (p. 380). This, then, is an instance of both infinite and paradoxical *mise en abyme:* the Unnamable is the x on both ends of the series, at once the anonymous narrator and the anonymous narrated of previous fictions, containing the long chain of lies that contain him (?). (Thus, the Unnamable asks: "que viens-je faire dans ces histoires de Mahood et de Worm, ou plutôt que viennent-ils faire dans la mienne..." [p. 183]. / "what am I doing in Mahood's story, and in Worm's, or rather what are they doing in mine..." [p. 377].) It is this labyrinthic prison of textual duplication, of doubling and redoubling fictions, of lying images and voices that is being sabotaged by the textual play. The narrator attacks the "hell of stories" by subverting narrative discourse from within, by undermining its shifting time,

---

c'est-à-dire le tissu des signifiants qui constitue l'œuvre, parce que le texte est l'affleurement même de la langue, et que c'est à l'intérieur de la langue que la langue doit être combattue, dévoyée: non par le message dont elle est l'instrument, mais par le jeu des mots dont elle est le théâtre."/ "By *literature* I mean ... the writing process. I therefore stress essentially the text in literature, that is, the texture of signifiers that constitute the work, because the text is the very surfacing of language, and because it is from inside language that language must be combatted, perverted: not by the message, of which it is the instrument, but by the play of words that it stages." (My translation.)

[41] In addition to the pits and cages already cited, other images of confinement proliferate in the text: "je suis emmuré de leurs vociférations" (p. 78) / "I am walled round with their vociferations" (p. 325); "Ce sera le cachot, c'est le cachot, ça a toujours été le cachot..." (pp. 167-68) / "They'll clap me in a dungeon, I'm in a dungeon, I've always been in a dungeon..." (p. 369); "je ne suis pas dehors, je suis dedans, dans quelque chose, je suis enfermé, le silence est dehors ... il me faut une prison ... j'y suis déjà..." (p. 253) / "I'm not outside, I'm inside, I'm in something, I'm shut up, the silence is outside ... I need a prison ... I'm there already..." (p. 410).

space, and person indicators, by refusing conventional narrative orientations and characterizations.

Although its horizontal texture sets it apart from the previous novels, *Comment c'est,* Beckett's seventh novel, repeats similar narrative game strategies. The text's metanarrative refrains, "je le dis comme je l'entends" / "I say it as I hear it" and "quelque chose là qui ne va pas" / "something wrong there," recall the long progression of narrators quoting snatches from fragmentary inner texts. Again, three instances of the voice chain (the first-person narrator and his doubles), here reduplicated by generations of witnesses and scribes, stretch into infinity: "et je suis là toujours été là avec Pim Bom d'innombrables autres dans une procession sans fin ni commencement" (p. 154) / "and there I am always was with Pim Bom innumerable others in a procession without end or beginning" (p. 127). Bom echoes the narrator who echoes Pim who echoes another, and so on: "je parle comme lui [Pim] Bom parlera comme moi qu'un parler ici l'un après l'autre la voix l'a dit" (p. 94). / "I talk like him [Pim] Bom will talk like me only one kind of talk here one after another the voice said so" (p. 76). And in an indirect reference to the previous novels, the narrator specifies that the present quoted text is one of six garbled versions (p. 162 / p. 134).

In *Comment c'est,* Beckett turns to modern sound and light reproduction media for his metaphors of self-duplication. In the previous year (1958), he had experimented with the tape recorder in *Krapp's Last Tape,* in which Krapp tapes in the present his voice commenting on his voice recorded in the past which speaks in turn of previous voice recordings. In the novel, the narrator imagines generations of voices reproduced on ebonite (p. 130 / p. 107), suggesting a multiplexed phonograph record.

On the other hand, the images the narrator evokes of life above in the light are compared to a cinema in the French version — "d'où me vient ce cinéma" (p. 39) — although the English translation, "whence this dumb show" (p. 32), makes it clear that the writer is punning on the word *cinéma* to suggest both film and fiction. (The English puns on the two meanings of "dumb," stupid and silent.) It is not surprising, then, that a few years after the novel, Beckett made a silent film, *Film* (first called "The Eye," a homophone of "I"), in which the camera (called E for eye) films an eye looking at a number of eyes including a series of photographed past eyes or I's and ending with the confrontation of the doubles eye to eye.[42]

In *Comment c'est* — and in *Krapp's Last Tape* and *Film* — instead of mirroring himself in the narrators by means of versions of his own name — Hackett, Sam, Lemuel — Beckett has the narrator/narrated confront scenes not only from past fictions, which are partly autobiographical, but from the author's own life, in certain instances recorded by actual photographs.[43] Thus, to describe the retrospective scenes, glimpsed through muddy obscurity, the novel's narrator, like those before him, alternates past and present tenses, since it is undetermined whether he quotes memory inscriptions or fictional representations. Or more precisely, the memory traces, whether stories or moving pictures, like so many clichés of a complex process, are as illusory as fiction. Thus, not only is fiction a past narrative, but the past is narrative fiction or a muddled lie. Consequently, the prints in *Film* are torn to bits, Krapp's tape reduced to silence, and the scenes in *Comment c'est* extinguished in the dark: there is no resurrection of the past, only flickering images and fading voices on and off.

Curiously, *Comment c'est*'s scenes from the past, simultaneously remembered and fictional, are imagined on the vertical plane as "above" — "TA VIE LA-HAUT" (p. 93) / "YOUR LIFE ABOVE" (p. 75) — and on the horizontal plane as "in front of" the eyes (the inner eyes). Thus, about people in an imagined scene involving a former self, the narrator says: "j'ai l'impression que nous me regardons" (p. 36). / "I have the impression we are looking at me" (p. 29). Semantically, this goes counter the usual French and English expressions of the past as located "behind" or stretched out "below." It has been pointed out that writing is one of the sources of the unexpected vertical expressions being discussed here, that is,

---

[42] The first title of the script is indicated by Alan Schneider, "On Directing *Film*," in *Film*, by Samuel Beckett (New York: Grove Press, 1969), p. 65.

[43] The famous photograph of Beckett at his mother's knee, first reproduced in *Beckett at Sixty* (London: Calder and Boyars, 1967), and Deirdre Bair's comments in *Samuel Beckett: A Biography* (New York: Harcourt Brace Jovanovich, 1978), pp. 521-22, make explicit Beckett's use of autobiographical material in the novel.

the textual directions "see the arguments presented below (later)" and "see above (earlier)" correspond to the "future-below" and "past-above" conceptualization. [44] And indeed, the scenes "above" in *Comment c'est* are not only earlier in relation to the narrator/narrated but also in a "see above" relationship to Beckettian texts. (The characters described as looking at the narrator, for example, resemble those of "Fingal" in *More Pricks than Kicks*.) Thus, the playful contestation of time categories that would imprison the infinite in linguistic time, is here extended from verb tense to the spatial expressions of temporal sequencing.

As one follows the succession of words on the syntagmatic plane, *Comment c'est* resembles a long sentence (like the ones in *L'Innommable*) which, however, after all interior punctuation has been removed, stretches out in both directions, leaving neither a beginning nor an end, so that the novel's syntax — one long sentence fragment — as well as the vertical and horizontal textual organization all work together to indicate a radical open-endedness. That Beckett had first thought of having the entire text printed without the blank spaces that now separate groups of words would seem to support this supposition. [45] The way in which the novel was finally printed, however, makes *Comment c'est* easier to read than *L'Innommable*, despite its lack of punctuation, since the gaps between fragments divide the text into what Barthes in *S/Z* calls lexies, the basic units of reading, which, in the novel, divide into phonetically determined rhythmic groups, which in turn contain patterns of sound repetitions. [46] Within each lexie, then, and from one to the other, sounds and refrains produce echoic patterns: "soudain au loin le pas la voix rien puis soudain quelque chose quelque chose puis soudain rien soudain au loin le silence" (p. 16) / "suddenly afar the step the voice nothing then suddenly something something then suddenly nothing suddenly afar the silence" (p. 13).

---

[44] See Elizabeth Closs Traugott, "Spatial Expressions of Tense and Temporal Sequencing," *Semiotica*, 15, No. 3 (1975), 223.

[45] See Deirdre Bair, p. 521.

[46] See Roland Barthes, "Le Texte étoilé," in *S/Z* (Paris: Seuil, 1970), pp. 20-21. In *Structuralist Poetics* (Ithaca: Cornell Univ. Press, 1975), p. 202, Jonathan Culler summarizes Barthes's definition as follows: "A lexie is a minimal unit of reading, a stretch of text which is isolated as having a specific effect or function different from that of neighboring stretches of text."

It is not surprising, therefore, that the alliteration, assonance, refrain-like repetition of rhythmic groups, and the verse-like pattern of fragments have brought many readers to compare the novel to poetry and music.[47]

As is apparent from the quotes from the novel, another modification of syntactic structure relates the text to poetry, that is, its extensive use of deletion transformations or ellipsis. Most striking in *Comment c'est* is the omission of the copula "to be"; subsequent texts will delete further function words — articles, subject pronouns, and so on — resulting in a type of telegraphic writing. In the past, in Joyce's *Ulysses*, for example, such elliptic writing served to set the character's mental discourse apart from the third-person narration and to mimic the discontinuities of direct thought quotation or interior monologue.[48] In *Comment c'est* and many of the short Beckettian texts of the sixties and seventies, the extensive use of syntactic deletions — in *Still*, for example, written in 1972, the subject pronoun "I" is omitted throughout — joins the other textual strategies in pointing to the fragmentary status of the series of inner texts, the multiple surface manifestations of an abysmal deep structure whose laws, whose relation to meaning are unfathomable.

Besides *Comment c'est*'s echoic and fragmented syntax, the novel's three horizontal divisions, so the narrator explains (pp. 141-42 / p. 116), repeat themselves endlessly: parts five, nine, thirteen, etc. reduplicate Part I (the journey); parts four, six, eight, and so on, redouble Part II (the couple); and parts seven, eleven, fifteen... duplicate Part III (the abandon). However, in place of the round song's (and *Godot*'s and *Play*'s) convolutions, these re-

---

[47] In *Samuel Beckett: A Study of His Novels* (London: Peter Owen, 1970), pp. 162-69, Eugene Webb likens *Comment c'est*'s compositional pattern to the sonata form. Ruby Cohn (*Back to Beckett*, pp. 226-40), classifying the novel under Beckett's "Lyrics of Fiction," refers to it as free verse. Both critics point out that Beckett's English translation of the text fails to transcribe many of the rhythmic cadences of the French.

[48] See, for example, *Ulysses* (London: The Bodley Head, 1966), p. 115: "Mr Bloom reviewed the nails of his left hand, then those of his right hand. The nails, yes. Is there anything more in him that they she sees? Fascination. Worst man in Dublin. That keeps him alive. They sometimes feel what a person is. Instinct. But a type like that. My nails. I am just looking at them: well pared. And after: thinking alone."

petitions set up an interminable to and fro between the solitary or abandoned and the couple states, moving from (1) journey to (2) couple to (3) abandon to (4) couple to (5) journey to (6) couple to (7) abandon to (8) couple, and so on. Nor is the order I, II, III fixed: the narrative could as easily begin with the abandon (Part III) or with the couple (Part II). (A few years later, in *Sans/Lessness*, dating from the late sixties, the order in which the 120 sentences appear was indeed left to chance. To compose the text, Beckett drew sentences he had written from a bag at random.)[49] In *Comment c'est*, then, the abysmal narrative structure of the novels from *Watt* through the Three Novels, is doubled by an infinite reduplication of the flawed horizontal surface in an unending play of self-deferment.

In concluding the first part on Beckettian narrative strategies, a chart ordering the various techniques reviewed would be useful. Ludovic Janvier has drawn up a table specifying whether or not each fiction's narrator participates in the action and indicating the presence or absence of the narrating instance in the text.[50] But then, from our analysis, it seems clear that the early Beckettian narrator's mode of being outside is contested by his metanarrative statements that he is really inside, that the first-person participations of the French narrators are first assured then denied, and that, in general, the third person is suspected of being a first person and the first person a third person, the two being, moreover, intertwined in novel after novel, and that the short prose pieces of the sixties and seventies use sometimes third-person, sometimes first-person narration (with the first-person deleted or not) — to mention only these aspects — and how is one to chart such devious narrating games?

Instead, in guise of a summary, a look at the textual devices at work in a short poem will serve to reemphasize the elements of Beckettian play:

> on all that strand
> at end of day
> steps sole sound

---

[49] See Ruby Cohn, *Back to Beckett*, pp. 265-66.
[50] See "Lieu dire," in *Cahier Samuel Beckett*, ed. Tom Bishop and Raymond Federman, *L'Herne*, No. 31 (1976), p. 195.

> long sole sound
> until unbidden stay
> then no sound
> on all that strand
> long no sound
> until unbidden go
> steps sole sound
> long sole sound
> on all that strand
> at end of day [51]

"Roundelay," written in 1976, contains thirteen lines with the end circling back to the beginning as demanded by the genre. (A slight deviation has the first line, which appropriately serves as refrain in the middle of the poem [line 7], reoccur in line 12, instead of 13.) Like the other round song, which so many Beckettian texts stage and mimic, "Roundelay" reduplicates itself endlessly. Unlike the song about the dog's tombstone, however, Beckett's poem has one verse, not two, nor does it contain a textual duplication within itself. Instead, "Roundelay" features a different echoic structure. Thus, the first two lines, taken together, repeated by the last two lines, establish a spatio-temporal frame around the brief narrative. (It is of note that this frame evokes two borders, between sea and land, and night and day.) Within this outer frame is embedded another, at the border of sound and silence, that is, lines 10 and 11 redouble lines 3 and 4: (1, 2 (3, 4   10, 11) 12, 13). Inside this second frame, lines 5 and 9 indicate motion and stasis: (1, 2 (3, 4 (5   9) 10, 11) 12, 13). Finally, the center embeds an abyss of silence. Over and over again, the poem retraces tracks made and effaced, made and effaced, to and from silence.

The poem's echoic structure is further reinforced by lexical, phonological, rhythmic, and syntactic patterns. The semantic oppositions of motion-stasis, light-dark, sound-silence are conveyed by a small number of monosyllabic words. Of these, only the "stay-go" contrast is evoked singly, whereas "at end of day" appears twice, and the "sole sound-no sound" antithesis several times over. On the phonological level, the alliteration of /s/ in "steps sole sound/long sole sound" and in most end of line words echoes

---

[51] "Roundelay," *Collected Poems in English and French* (New York: Grove Press, 1977), p. 35.

the soft slur of steps muffled by the consonance of /nd/ at line end. And the repetition of the nasal consonants /n/ and /ŋ/ together with the liquid /l/, all associated with softness, as well as the large number of sonorous vowels and dipthongs /o/ /ɔ/ /æ/ /aw/ contribute to the poem's musical effects or the pre-symbolic pleasure of sound play.[52] Rhythmic contrasts, on the other hand, serve to underscore the poem's to and fro: the quickest tempo is reserved for the motion-stasis frame, whereas, inside and outside it, the sound-silence lines slow to three long beats.

Finally, syntactic parallelism reinforces the poem's phonological and semantic symmetries and asymmetries. Thus, the poem's only verbs "stay-go" foreground the motion-stasis opposition and, in addition, indicate that the ronudelay is conceived in the iterative or repeated present tense. Most striking are the poem's syntactic deletions — punctuation, definite articles, copulas (at [the] end of [the] day/steps [are] [the] sole sound) and subject pronouns ([they?] [I?] stay) — which fragment the surface texture.

In this brief poem, then, as throughout the novels, the echoic textual patterns as well as the horizontal and vertical narrative reduplications, like the embedded *fort/da* games at the border of light and dark, sound and silence, motion and stasis, and finally, of sense and no sense, serve to fracture the symbolic order by their abysmal play.

---

[52] In my analysis of sound patterns, I follow Geoffrey N. Leech, *A Linguistic Guide to English Poetry* (London: Longmans, 1969), pp. 89-100.

Part II

THEMATIC REDUPLICATION

The playful repetitions inscribed in the narrative structure of the novels can now be examined thematically. Most helpful for a reading of Beckett's esthetic games is to compare them with the psychoanalytic play techniques developed by Melanie Klein. Klein would offer her young patients a choice of toys which, as they began to play with them, would take on a variety of symbolic meanings bound up with their phantasies, wishes, and experiences. The child analyst would then interpret the symbolic language of play, whether a *mise en scène* of toys or an acting out through role-playing, a type of psycho-drama she also encouraged, in order to arrive at the child's unconscious conflicts.[1]

Along similar lines, Beckett is said to have been impressed by C. G. Jung's contention that "you can read a writer's mind when you study the characters he creates." Jung presented this approach to reading during the third of his Tavistock lectures, the one Beckett attended in 1935.[2] It is important to note, however, that what Klein and Jung perceive as the child's or the writer's un-

---

[1] See Melanie Klein, "The Psycho-Analytic Play Technique: Its History and Significance" (1955), in *Envy and Gratitude and Other Works*, 1946-63 ([New York]: Delacorte Press, 1975), pp. 122-40; and "Personification in the Play of Children" (1929), in *Love, Guilt and Reparation and Other Works*, 1921-1945 (London: Hogarth Press, 1975), pp. 199-209.

[2] See Deirdre Bair, *Samuel Beckett: A Biography*, p. 208; and C. G. Jung, *Analytical Psychology: The Tavistock Lectures* (New York: Pantheon Books, 1968), p. 81. In the third lecture, as well, Jung (p. 92) compares his method of dream analysis to the method a philologist would apply in reading a text in an unknown language or a fragmentary text.

conscious process of dramatization is the very material of Beckett's narrative games: on the thematic level, the undoing of conflicts, and on the narrative level, the play with play, or the writer as analyst-reader of his own mental *mise en scène*.

In Beckett's games, we find, then, that the narrators manipulate a number of toys which are recognizably the same, although visibly deteriorated or damaged from one novel to the next: nested figures (fragmented parts of the narrators) and items of clothing — hats, coats, boots — which are put on and off; a number of instruments and containers whose sexual symbolic meaning is invariable, umbrellas, sticks, rulers, can-openers, cords, ladders, crutches, pencils and pens, notebooks, bags, and sacks which are alternately lost and found. In addition, the Beckettian toybox-psyche includes houses divided into rooms with rocking chairs and beds as their most important furnishings, and landscapes of gardens, woods, plains near seashore and mountains, roads and towns, canals and rivers traversed by trams, trains, carriages, bicycles, and boats. And one must not forget a whole menagerie of domesticated and wild animals, mostly dogs, hens, parrots, goats, lambs, pigs, cows, horses, rats too, and bees and wild birds which come and go through light and dark. In the novels, though, most importantly, it is not the objects themselves but the words that name them that ultimately are the elements of the game.

Each narrator rearranges his toys into repeated symmetric patterns which, like so many chess pieces, are each time scattered until the next round of play. Or like the little boy in *Beyond the Pleasure Principle* or the old man in *Malone meurt* — both meditations on Thanatos — the toys are made to disappear and reappear. What are the symmetric patterns? And what conflicts do they stage? The texts themselves, as will become clear, suggest that the opposing positions inscribed in the novels can be correlated to a large number of polarities, cosmological, mythic, religious, philosophical, psychological, and to writing itself. What makes Beckett's novels such inexhaustible texts is partly that they produce codes of such symbolic force that they seem to call up the entire semantic universe which through the ages has been applied to the human condition. Finally, though, as we know, the meanings are only played with like so many toys. Beckett's language of play yields repeated symbolic readings which are then demystified by the game itself. Meaning is always postponed or deferred. Nevertheless, before they undermine their symbolic forms of play, the texts transform the semantic material they play with and produce intriguing versions of the old myths staging the basic contraries of existence.

In his first novel, Beckett inscribed several games which reduplicate the work's narrative and thematic conflicts. Unlike the future novels, *Murphy*, which is still written largely from the omniscient perspective, is not framed by the *fort/da* game, the narrator's own game with words. Instead, the games in this novel function as a thematic *mise en abyme*. (The exception is Miss Carridge's brief fiction in Chapter viii which mimics the narrating.) In particular, the famous chess game for which the narrator lists eighty-six moves, followed by eighteen metatextual notes, mirrors the narrative in miniature, for by following the moves of the game we obtain a condensation of the conflicts staged by *Murphy*. Together with Murphy's horoscope of Chapter iii, and the kites of Chapter xiii, the chess game of Chapter xi thus functions as an interior duplication of the novel.[3] Indeed, Beckett had considered placing the game of chess into an epilogue in a section by itself, perhaps as he was to affix the addenda to *Watt*, as a commentary on the novel.[4]

In order to show how the game of chess parodies the novel, the principal conflicts *Murphy* stages need to be summarized. The novel's narrator, as we have seen oscillates between the posture of authorial sovereignty, pulling strings or positioning pieces, and the modest anonymity of mouthpiece and reflection of an inner persona. Murphy, the narrator's persona, wavers similarly between the poles of autonomous and anonymous subject, between a Cartesian and post-Cartesian order. Tied to his rocking chair, Murphy moves in place in quest of an original proximity to self,

---

[3] In *Samuel Beckett's "Murphy": A Critical Excursion* (Athens: Univ. of Georgia Press, 1968), p. 73 ff., Robert Harrison outlines how the horoscope "paraphrases in pseudo-astrological argot the dramatic events of the book." For other readings of the chess game, see Robert Harrison, pp. 77-79; John Fletcher and John Spurling, *Beckett: A Study of His Plays* (New York: Hill and Wang, 1972), pp. 30-33; and Deirdre Bair, pp. 220-21 and 224-25.

[4] See Samuel Beckett, Letter to Thomas McGreevy, 17 July 1936, in *Samuel Beckett: A Biography*, by Deirdre Bair, p. 228.

letting the puppets or pawns of the novel execute complex figures in his pursuit. They desire Murphy who desires himself. In following up the narrator's own suggestions, the motions of the characters may be drafted onto a triangle inscribed in a circle.[5] The lines of desire lead to the unwilling Murphy in Narcissus-position at the center. And while the movements of desire keep changing direction, they do so without breaking the pattern of triangular desires within a circle:

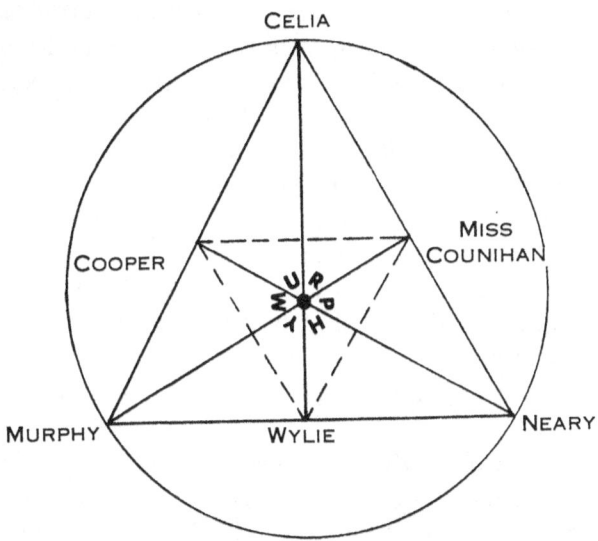

Murphy desires Murphy; for the others he exists at the intersection of their need and desire. As best illustrated by the Neary-Murphy relationship, he is both end and key to the end. First, Neary desires Murphy as a means to Miss Counihan. Then, Murphy from rival becomes the end; Celia becomes the means to Murphy. Thirdly, Celia in turn evolves from means to end and "restored Murphy from being an end in himself to his initial condition of

---

[5] "Murphy then is actually being needed by five people outside himself" (p. 202); and "'Remember there is no triangle, however obtuse, but the circumference of some circle passes through its wretched vertices.'... 'Our medians,' said Wylie, 'or whatever the hell they are, meet in Murphy'" (p. 213).

obstacle (or key)" (p. 257). In a similar vein, the author turns the Racinian ladder of desire into a reversible circle and exaggerates it to the point of parody: "Of such was Neary's love for Miss Dwyer, who loved a Flight-Lieutenant Elliman, who loved a Miss Farren of Ringsakiddy, who loved a Father Fitt of Ballinclashet, who in all sincerity was bound to acknowledge a certain vocation for Mrs. West of Passage, who loved Neary" (p. 5).

Murphy wants to break out of the triangle by desiring only himself, out of the circle through "the short circuit" of requited love (p. 29). But the two ways are irreconcilable: either Narcissus or Eros. (A similar conflict informs the Belacqua stories in which Eros loses to Narcissus.) For Murphy, life with Celia (both whore and celestial),[6] who "suggested that he might try his hand at something more remunerative than apperceiving himself into a glorious grave" (p. 21), would mean the loss of self to the other, that is, the body, in extension to the "slave-markets" of work (p. 77), or to celestial determination, in short to what alienates the self and determines it as other. Yet Murphy, much more so than Belacqua, would have liked to reconcile Eros and Narcissus. He regretfully gives up Celia.

Unable to resolve the conflict between self and other, Murphy replaces Eros and celestial transcendence by self-transcendence. It is a *retreat* into interiority. For example, when Murphy in search for a job elicits the comment, " 'E don't look rightly human to me' " (p. 77), the experience of his non-entity in the world overpowers him. Incapable of human posture, he feels the need for the rocking-chair-cradle. The failure to be recognized by the other, that is, his nothingness, determines his repudiation of the world: " 'I am not of the big world, I am of the little world' was an old refrain with Murphy, and a conviction, two convictions, the negative first" (p. 178). Nothing in the outer world, he withdraws into the inner "where he could love himself" (p. 7). In order not to let the world

---

[6] The narrator-author plays on the name of Celia through suggestions of "celestial" and *s'il y a* (pp. 7 and 117). Her profession gives rise to indirect puns on "horoscope." In addition, the indication that Murphy as a theological student "used to lie awake night after night with Bishop Bouvier's *Supplementum ad Tractatum de Matrimonio* under his pillow" (p. 72) further underlines the affinity between woman and celestial transcendence in the novel.

overpower him, he chooses self-idolatry. Thus, the heading of Chapter vi, "*Amor intellectualis quo Murphy se ipsum amat,*" twists Spinoza's Proposition 35 in Part V of the *Ethics* where it applies to God.

Thus, Murphy recalls both Narcissus and Descartes. For through Murphy, who "felt himself split in two, a body and a mind" (p. 109), Beckett ridicules the Cartesian heritage. Murphy, tied into his rocking-chair to quiet his body in order to move unfettered in his mind, is a humorous version of Descartes who, settled in his stove, sought to guide his mind along the proper road to the indubitable truth of his existence. But, whereas in the *Discours de la méthode,* Descartes carefully circumvented the pitfalls in the path to the *cogito,* Murphy constantly falls back into the world of the senses he is trying to leave behind: the telephone's ring calls him back to Celia; the rocking-chair topples him, nose to the ground. He finds it impossible to reach the *cogito.*

The narrator gives us an inside view of Murphy's mind in Chapter vi. This sphere pictures itself divided into three zones, light, half light, and dark, which correspond roughly to consciousness, self-consciousness, and the unconscious. The first region contains "the world of the body broken up into the pieces of a toy" (p. 112) and the possibility of revenge; the second, peaceful contemplation; the third, an unknowable infinity, a "[m]atrix of surds" (p. 112). It is striking that in this piece of psycho-narration, the narrator does not reveal intimate thoughts and feelings but pictures the mind as the stage of conflicts among fragmented parts of the self spoken of in terms of toys, of mirror images, and finally of indecipherable forces, all linked to light and darkness.

The triple alternatives existed for Belacqua as well, who like Murphy was "trine.... Centripetal, centrifugal and ... not. Phoebus chasing Daphne, Narcissus flying from Echo and ... neither." In a regressive move, Belacqua would recede from Eros to Narcissus and from Narcissus to Thanatos or the "wombtomb":

> The third being [besides Phoebus and Narcissus] was the dark gulf, when the glare of the will and the hammer-strokes of the brain doomed outside to take flight from its quarry were expunged, the Limbo and the wombtomb alive with the unanxious spirits of quiet cerebration, where

there was no conflict of flight and flow and Eros was as null as Anteros and Night had no daughters.[7]

"When the mind went wombtomb,"[8] in the dark of the psyche, one experiences the state that Murphy terms, "[s]o pleasant that pleasant was not the word" (p. 113).

Belacqua's and Murphy's wombtomb phantasy can indeed be related to the Freudian pleasure principle, which seeks to reduce outer and inner excitations to zero, and which Freud linked with the Nirvana principle and identified with the death instincts.[9] (The term "Nirvana," first proposed by the English psychoanalyst Barbara Low in the present context, points to Hindu and Buddhistic religious concepts and to Schopenhauer who popularized the word in the West.)[10] Consequently, the repeated references to will-lessness and desire-lessness in the Belacqua stories and *Murphy,* joined to a regressive "enwombing" motif, connect Belacqua's and Murphy's third psychic topos with the psychoanalytic Nirvana concept and Thanatos.[11] "Pleasant," then, is indeed not the word. Nor is this the last time that a Beckettian text will cite the Freudian pleasure principle. Moran in *Molloy,* most appropriately, calls it "le funeste principe du plaisir" (p. 153)/ "the fatal pleasure principle" (p. 99).

That Beckett chose to stage the clash between the first two psychic zones in terms of Eros and Narcissus, the mythic figures

---

[7] The two excerpts are from "Dream of Fair to Middling Women," pp. 107-08, as quoted in *Samuel Beckett: Poet and Critic,* by Lawrence E. Harvey (Princeton: Princeton Univ. Press, 1970), p. 269 and p. 326. Ellipsis points and interpolation in brackets as in Harvey.

[8] Quoted from "Dream," in Harvey, p. 326.

[9] See *Beyond the Pleasure Principle* (1920), in *Standard Edition,* XVIII, 55-56; and "The Economic Problem of Masochism" (1924), in *Collected Papers,* trans. Joan Riviere (New York: Basic Books, 1959), II, 255-57.

[10] See Jean Laplanche and J.-B. Pontalis, "Principe de Nirvana," in *Vocabulaire de la psychanalyse* (Paris: P.U.F., 1967), pp. 331-32. This reference work has been translated as *The Language of Psychoanalysis* (New York: Norton, 1973).

[11] The word "enwombing" comes from "Dream," p. 162, as quoted by Harvey, p. 262. The Schopenhauerian traces in Beckett are pointed out by Harvey on p. 325, n. 6: "The recurrent indictment of desire, need, and will demonstrates the affinity between the views of Schopenhauer and those of Beckett."

preferred by psychoanalytic discourse, is striking as well.[12] In *Murphy*, as we have seen, narcissism is further linked to the philosophy of introspection and dualism: the Cartesian *cogito* repeats the Narcissus myth through its reduplication of consciousness — I think/I am. On the other hand, Narcissus represents the rejection of others for love of self. Finally, however, the desire of Narcissus to become one with his reflected image in the water points to a Nirvana motif: ultimately, Narcissus aims to reenter the oneness of the womb also identified with death.[13] Eros versus Narcissus is finally Eros versus Thanatos.

In returning to the chess game in *Murphy*, we see that it functions like another psychic metaphor, as it were, giving another view of Murphy's mind as it humorously and drastically turns the Cartesian *cogito* into a narcissistic version of the mythic game of chess with death.

Mr. Endon, Murphy's partner at chess, is a schizophrenic in the mental asylum in which Murphy has taken a job, or more precisely, has taken refuge. The mental asylum, reappearing in several Beckettian novels, is clearly an image of interiority, and *endon*, as often pointed out, is Greek for "within." Within this inner space, then, Mr. Endon, a royal and Buddha-like figure (later resurrected in the Hamm of *Endgame*), dressed in black inside and scarlet outside, has achieved the immediacy of self in the mental twilight. Mr. Endon's impenetrability, however, does not exclude at least one temptation, suicide, and one "frivolity," chess (p. 187). During the day, Murphy would interrupt his duties in the wards, Mr. Endon his drifting about, to make their moves on the chessboard, mostly in the absence of the other player. Since Mr. Endon avoided any direct confrontation and Murphy imitated his opponent, neither player would lose a piece or even check the

---

[12] Laplanche and Pontalis — "Narcissisme," p. 263 — indicate that Havelock Ellis first described perverse autoerotic behavior in relation to the Narcissus myth in his *Autoerotism: A Psychologcial Study* (1898). Freud and others followed his lead.

[13] Freud refers to this regressive component as primary narcissism which, together with primary masochism, is undistinguishable from the death or Nirvana instinct. See "The Economic Problem of Masochism," in *Collected Papers*, II, 255-68; and Laplanche and Pontalis, "Narcissisme primaire, narcissisme secondaire," p. 264.

other after eight or nine hours of play. Such "Fabian" tactics (named after Quintus Fabius Maximus, the 3rd century B. C. Roman general who defeated Hannibal by avoiding direct conflict) again prevail during the famous game played by Murphy and Mr. Endon during Murphy's first and last assignment of night duty in Chapter xi.

Unlike the previous games out in the ward, this match is played in Mr. Endon's cell face to face. We already know that Murphy imitates Endon's tactis, and the text bristles with other examples of his identification with the schizophrenic. In order to make it quite clear, though, the narrator indicates that Murphy felt drawn to Mr. Endon's psychosis "as Narcissus to his fountain" (p. 186). These clues and an analysis of the moves of the chess game bring us to the discovery that this astonishing game is played as if in a mirror, and moreover, not only in one mirror, but in two. Murphy struggles to reflect each move of his opponent, to maintain the original specular alignment of chess, white mirroring black. Mr. Endon, however, seemingly ignoring the opposite side of the board, is intent on setting up his mirror at right angles to it, maintaining the further chess mirror formation of the Black King's side reflecting the Black Queen's. His is a game of chess embedded within a game of chess, a mirror game within a mirror game.

We are now ready to examine the game's intricate structure more closely. Murphy, we have been told in a previous chapter, always played White; Mr. Endon, the first annotation of the game informs us, only played Black. Obviously, in this unusual game, playing White is the first disadvantage. Murphy, seemingly oblivious to the Fabian tactics adopted in previous matches, reverts to a standard offensive opening. His Pawn to King 4, however, does not evoke the expected defensive response by Black. Why should it? Endon's strategy consists of playing outside the trivial offensive/defensive maneuvers of chess. Black therefore begins his "Affence, or *Zweispringerspott*" (p. 243) by moving Knight to King's Rook 3.[14] White copies Black's move. Black moves Rook to King's

---

[14] The first play on words, "Affence," underscores and negates the offensive/defensive dimension of chess. The second, *Zweispringerspott*, points to and mocks the *Dreispringerspiel*, a well-known opening.

Knight 1. White mimics Black. The mirror games have began in earnest.

The two self-reflexive games, Murphy's with Endon (his specular double), Endon's in turn with himself, soon encounter insuperable barriers, so that eventually each player loses his game. Murphy's game runs into difficulty first: following Black's fourth move, White is prevented by his Pawn at King 4 from duplicating the move. (A note appropriately pointed out that White's offensive opening play would cause all his subsequent difficulties.) Since, in the game that follows, White falls more and more behind in his mimicry, Murphy struggles madly either to emulate Endon or to surrender his Knight, Queen, Bishop, and King and failing in both maneuvers, to revert to trivial strategies of defense and attack. The narrator's notes clearly favor Black's esthetic moves and mock White's tactics, as for example in note (p): "No words can express the torment of mind that goaded White to this abject offensive" (p. 245).

Endon, in the meanwhile, plays his game of "solitaire" (note q) moving the pieces on his side of the board in accordance with esthetic rules of symmetry and dissymmetry, displacing them only to replace them into a series of mirror reflections, aiming eventually to recover the original order. As Deirdre Bair writes, Endon's game is "based on the assumption that a piece should not be moved unless it can be returned safely to its original position" (op. cit., pp. 220-21). At the end of his eighth move, Black has returned his pieces to their initial symmetrical position, an accomplishment praised in note (d): "An ingenious and beautiful début, sometimes called the Pipe-opener" (p. 244). Subsequently, moves 21, 23, 27, 39, and 41 place Black's pieces into specular patterns, the Black Queen's and Black King's sides of the board reflecting each other. Nor are these numbers chosen haphazardly. To the contrary, they figure in a further mathematical game of reduplication: [15]

---

[15] I am indebted to Kishin Moorjani for solving this mathematical puzzle and for his discussion of chess strategies.

$$8 = 2^3$$
$$21 = 3 \times 2^3 - 3$$
$$23 = 3 \times 2^3 - 1$$
$$27 = 3 \times 2^3 + 3$$

$$39 = 2(3 \times 2^3 - 3) - 3$$
$$41 = 2(3 \times 2^3 - 3) - 1$$
$$[45 = 2(3 \times 2^3 - 3) + 3]$$

Number 45 would have rounded out the pattern of reduplication. The game ends quite unexpectedly after the forty-third play, however. To understand why, we must examine the final moves.

Murphy had attempted at first to mirror each move of his opponent, and then like Narcissus, to solicit recognition from his reflection in the glass. Mr. Endon, however, gives no sign of perceiving his opponent's game. Note (o), for example, informs us that Mr. Endon did not cry "Check!" nor give "the slightest indication that he was alive to having attacked the King of his opponent" (p. 245), and, of course, he takes none of the pieces White offers him. Then, just as according to the rules of chess (carefully followed by both players throughout), White is in a position to attack his opponent's own mirror game by preventing the return of Black's King to the starting position, in final mimicry of Mr. Endon's refusal to cry "Check" after move 34, Murphy resigns the game after move 43 by laying his King on his side.

The recurrent insistence on containment (the board in set up on Endon's bed, in his cell, in the asylum) and on the clash between offensive/defensive strategies on the one hand and self-reflexive play on the other, as well as on darkness (the game is played at night; Endon is dressed largely in black, plays only Black against Black) recalls the regions of Murphy's mind. Murphy's preference recedes from the light zone (revenge) to the twilight (self-reflection) to the dark ("pleasure"). And indeed, in following through the movement from consciousness to self-consciousness to the unconscious, after his surrender, Murphy loses consciousness and experiences nothingness, that is, the absence of being perceived, the text emphasizes, the absence of *percipi* rather than *percipere,* termed "a rare postnatal treat" (p. 246). Then, in resurfacing in the opposite direction, Murphy repeats the self-reflexive game by making himself appear and disappear directly in Mr. Endon's eyes. In this mirror, however, Murphy, unseen by Mr. Endon just as during the game, is therefore unseen by himself. And Murphy's death follows the same night, for Murphy finds that total unperceivedness is Nirvana, but perceiving himself as unperceived is death. He faces the mirror of death.

Thus, Murphy, failing to recognize the game as play and illusion, dies like Narcissus. Indeed, the series of introspective games, each a version of the self watching the self watching the self, bring to mind the *for/da* game in which the child makes himself disappear and reappear in the mirror in order to master the fear of his own disappearance when unperceived. We can now see that this form of mirror chess substitutes for the possible interactions on the board a suicidal pact. One of the players will be forced into the "gone" position, the unperceived position in the child's game with the mirror. In Murphy's version of the game, Mr. Endon would seem to possess the ultimate strategy. Like the Roman general who defeated Hannibal, is Mr. Endon, who wins by seemingly refusing to play, not all along only hiding his game? For why does he need a partner, why play his exquisite set of solitaire under the eyes of Murphy? Obviously, Mr. Endon needs to maneuver the others into witnessing his refusal to witness anyone but himself. The eyes of others reflect his supremacy, whereas his eyes mirror their nothingness. That Mr. Endon is suicidal only underscores his illusory omnipotence: without the other, he would fade away. A master of esthetics, a figure of the narcissistic artist, Mr. Endon deploys his tactics to assure the presence of admiring eyes upon him. Finally, however, although he defeats Murphy, Endon loses his own game with the mirror, for, without a partner to continue the match, his topsy-turvy King (turned upside down after move 30) cannot return to complete the symmetrical order. The suspended game leaves the King in a displaced position. Instead of one loser, there are two.

Since on the novel's thematic level, Endon is to Murphy what Murphy is to others, it becomes obvious that Murphy's apparent autonomy and flight from others are but a version of the same strategy of playing at not playing in order to win the game which, however, is but the game of death, life's game lost. Murphy's desire for himself (like Endon's for himself) depends on the desire of others, is but a reflection of the desire of others: he loves himself because they love him. Thus, in cutting the lines to them, he cuts the connection to himself. Therefore, before he dies, Murphy resolves (too late) to return to Celia, to reverse the movement of his flight, to give up mirror chess, the illusory glass of self.

Beckett's early fiction had staged the drama of desire by pitting Eros against Thanatos in similar ways. The personae, fearing to lose themselves in others, reverse their movement toward into flight from them. Since Eros, they feared, was death of self in the other, they preferred love of self and ultimately desire-lessness: Eros, Narcissus, Nirvana. Thus, the anonymous protagonist of "Assumption" (1929), Beckett's first piece of published fiction, whose voice was that of a man "who can reply confidently to Pawn to King's fourth, but whose faculties are frozen into bewildered suspension by Pawn to Rook's third," as silent listener to the conversations of others, oscillates between the offensive/defensive positions of either "whispering the turmoil down," submerging all into his silence, or losing himself in the fullness of their sound. Escaping from this struggle, he flees into narcissistic isolation and self-idolatry leading to dissolution of self and finally death. Belacqua's flight, as we have seen, follows a similar trajectory toward death. But whereas in *Murphy,* Celia is on the side of Eros, in the previous works, women are erotically devalued in order to fulfill the function of fountain of death. Thus, in "Assumption," the woman's eyes are "pools of obscurity," and at the end of "Walking Out" of *More Pricks than Kicks,* after Lucy is crippled and disfigured, Belacqua "finds in her big eyes better worlds than this." [16] In the early works, the eyes of women are the narcissistic mirror of death.

In choosing chess, the ancient game based on strategies of war, and turning it into an introspective mirror of inner conflicts, Beckett points to what precipitates the early protagonists' flight into death. Murphy's mind, Chapter vi informs us, is but an interiorized version of exteriority: "Nothing ever had been, was or would be in the universe outside it but was already present as virtual, or actual, or virtual rising into actual, or actual falling into virtual, in the universe inside it" (p. 107). As such, the retreat

---

[16] "Assumption" was published in *transition* [Paris], Nos. 16-17 (June 1929), pp. 268-71.

from offensive/defensive tactics during the game and Murphy's preference for non-violent zones of the mind parallel protagonist's flight from the reciprocal hostility of relations without. And reciprocal violence — making each person alternately victim and aggressor — is a major preoccupation from the 1929 "Assumption" and more strikingly the 1932 story "Dante and the Lobster," whose McCabe combines Abel and Cain, to the couples of *Comment c'est,* the symbiotic pairs of the plays, and the violence raging in the *Dépeupleur*'s cylinder.

As *Murphy* so clearly shows, however, strategic maneuvres, Fabian tactics, and flight are all of no avail against the power of Thanatos. By means of the ingenious game of mirror chess (really a series of embedded games), Beckett mocks Endon's, Murphy's, and, by extension, the narrator's Cartesian projects of an unmediated perception of self by showing that the intellectual love with which Murphy loved himself is but an "apperceiving himself into a glorious grave" (p. 21), Narcissus's game of chess with death.

The figures of the King, the sovereign author, the narcissistic artist, and the autonomous subject of rational philosophy all topple with *Murphy.* An old logocentric order explodes. *Murphy*'s esoteric chess game, an interior duplication of the novel containing a further reduplication of itself within itself, stages the displacement of the subject, of the kingly position of the self and its doubles, esthetic narcissism and authorial sovereignty. The undermining of the subject, which Freud announced and which the deconstructive criticism of the latter half of the twentieth century has been pursuing, is replayed by all of Beckett's texts from *Murphy* on.

To what extent *Murphy* ridicules one of the early Beckett's own positions is clear from the theoretical essays of the early thirties which more or less critically extol esthetic narcissism. Thus, Proust's art is "the apotheosis of solitude" and a 1934 article on a translation of Rilke speaks of "that prime article of Rilkean faith, which provides for the interchangeability of Rilke and God." [17] Beckett's early lyrical writing follows a similar path. The poems that frame *Echo's Bones* (1935), for example, suggest a narcissistic version of artistic sublimation. In "The Vulture," the

---

[17] *Proust,* p. 47; and rev. of *Poems,* by Rainer Maria Rilke, *The Criterion* [London], 13 (July 1934), 706.

first of the thirteen poems, Goethe's bird of prey which, like the poet's song, searches for fodder is placed within a psychic space.[18] The poet's mind, containing both vulture and world ("dragging his hunger through the sky/of my skull shell of sky and earth") must sacrifice itself, fracture and butcher its tissue (both are implied by the word "offal"), and at the same time mock the vulture by repudiating its hunger, by denying the poem's right to come into being: "mocked by a tissue that may not serve/till hunger earth and sky be offal." Consequently, "Echo's Bones," the short title poem placed at the end of the collection, suggests that as in the story of Echo, the nymph spurned by Narcissus, the bones, "taken by the maggots for what they are," that is the offal, the suffering fragments that make up the other poems of the collection, will give way to a disembodied echoing voice endlessly reverberating in the poet's psyche-asylum: ("asylum under my tread all this day"). Thus, the frame poems of *Echo's Bones* intimate narcissistic deliverance from the conflicts inscribed in its poems.

That what the writer mocks in his fiction are his own impulses is further evident from a letter written to his friend Thomas McGreevy, dated 10 March 1935, in which Beckett links the recurring depression and illnesses that plagued him after 1930 and which had led to two years in psychoanalysis under the care of W. R. Bion in London (1934-35) to his tendency to isolate himself. He had more and more "lent [him]-self to a crescendo of disengagement of others and [him]self," he wrote, and for a time the "misery and solitude and apathy" appeared to him "an index of superiority," until he was forced to acknowledge that his cultivation of "arrogant 'otherness'" was but a denial of life: "It was not until that way of living, or rather negation of living, developed such terrifying physical symptoms that it could no longer be pursued, that I became aware of anything morbid in myself."[19]

---

[18] Lawrence E. Harvey first linked Beckett's vulture with the poem-vulture of Goethe's "Harzreise im Winter" / "Winter Journey to the Harz Mountains." See his "Samuel Beckett: Initiation du poète," in *Configuration Critique de Samuel Beckett*, ed. Melvin J. Friedman (Paris: Minard, 1964), pp. 164-65; trans. and rpt. as "A Poet's Initiation," in *Samuel Beckett Now*, ed. M. J. Friedman (Chicago: Univ. of Chicago Press, 1970), pp. 183-84. See also Harvey's *Samuel Beckett: Poet and Critic*, pp. 112-16.

[19] Quoted in Bair, p. 198.

Since at the time of this self-analysis Beckett was writting *Murphy*, it becomes evident that the writer's major change of mind generated the novel's comic undermining of self-transcendence, the esoteric game of chess.

Just how important Beckett considered the chess game is apparent from a 13 November 1936 letter to George Reavy in which he refuses to give permission to have it cut.[20] Another letter, dated 17 July of the same year to Thomas McGreevy, as already mentioned, indicates that Beckett thought of placing the game into an epilogue. Instead, Chapter xiii of *Murphy* pictures kites at the end of their strings disappearing and reappearing, the "ludicrous fever of toys struggling skyward" (p. 281), a different version of *fort/da*. Thus, Mr. Kelly "could measure the distance from the unseen to the seen, now he was in a position to determine the point at which seen and unseen met" (p. 280). In a repetition of Murphy's losing game, a child's tandem of coupled kites crashes to earth, and Mr. Kelly's kite, to the dismay of its owner, disappears into the sky with its string. Both players, the child and the old man, fail to control the precarious play of seen and unseen, come and go. The games in *Murphy* thus end badly and sadly despite the comic and ironic tenor of the novel, for they reenact the loss of the symbolic object, the loss of other and therefore of self.

We can now compare the inner reduplication games of *Murphy* with those of *Watt*. Whereas the *fort/da* versions of *Murphy* result in a resounding "gone" leading the persona into an untimely death, a suicidal pining away before the mirror, in *Watt,* at the end of the mirror series, the game is not lost but to be continued, yet to begin. The myth of the autonomous subject exploded with *Murphy* and is usurped in *Watt* by a question, an unidentified image and voice fading away. And the narrators play discontinuous series of mirror and echo games with anonymous traces within.

Watt, written during World War II in Roussillon, is "only a game," a means of "staying sane," Beckett told Lawrence Harvey.[21] As previously pointed out, thematically the novel's embedded

---

[20] Quoted in Bair, p. 243.
[21] *Samuel Beckett: Poet and Critic,* p. 222.

games can be linked to a retrospective testing of the philosophical categories that through the ages have been applied to the human condition. Is it surprising that a writer whose usual apolitical stance had given way in the face of the horrors of World War II to active political resistance, a writer who had narrowly escaped violent death because of his Resistance activities in Paris and who after his flight to Roussillon continued with the *maquis*, would want to question the monuments of Western thought? Playfully, the novel tries these out and then dismantles one after the other.

To begin with the most archaic, the narratives embedded within Watt's narrative (Arsene's statement in Part I, the tale of the dog in Part II, and Arthur's story of the mathematical hoax in Part III, to which can be added the threne and the painting of the first two parts), reiterate the themes of incommensurability, of the one and the many, of union and disunion, being and becoming in terms reminiscent of the pre-Socratics. Do numbers, so these texts would ask, explain the cosmos? How thoroughly the mathematical spoofs — the lists, series, combinations, and permutations, which make up such a large part of *Watt*, are not only imperfect, but more importantly, have no relation to reality has been pointed out by John J. Mood.[22] At the end of the most grotesque of these games of exhaustive description, after twenty-four pages on the subject of bringing together a hypothetical dog and the left-overs of Mr Knott's meal — equally hypothetical — the narrator concludes: "Not that for a moment Watt supposed that he had penetrated the forces at play, in this particular instance, or even perceived the forms that they upheaved, or obtained the least useful information concerning himself, or Mr Knott, for he did not" (p. 117). Similarly, the number 52.285714285714 at the beginning of the threne, that is, the number of days in a week divided into the number of days in a year plus one day — total discourse — like pi continues endlessly. Hugh Kenner has discussed the importance of such irrational numbers

---

[22] "'The Personal System' — Samuel Beckett's *Watt*," pp. 255-65. Of thirty-seven items examined, Mood found faults in twelve. He considers these errors, as well as other frequent mistakes in the novel, planned: the faults in the form, repeating the failure portrayed in the plot, illustrate Beckett's despair of adequate expression, rational or otherwise.

in Beckett's works and convincingly linked this aspect to the Pythagoreans who considered irrational numbers a scandal.[23]

On the other hand, Arsene's prophetic statement (Arsene's name suggests a seer) describes what happens "to us all ... if only we chose to know it" (p. 45) in terms of the one and the many.[24] Arsene first recalls a state of cosmic immanence, of total unity: "I was in the sun, and the wall was in the sun. I was the sun, need I add, and the wall, and the step, and the yard, and the time of the year, and the time of the day, to mention only these" (p. 42). A sudden shift splinters the oneness into self and other. Arsene compares this "slip" to a "reversed metamorphosis" and to a fall caused by the removal of a ladder: "What was changed was existence off the ladder. Do not come down the ladder, Ifor, I haf taken it away" (p. 44).

Existence off the ladder, a fallen existence, a broken circle, is Watt's and the basic human experience. Moving backward in Part I to the time preceding Watt's arrival at Mr Knott's, we first encounter Watt as a load left by a tram that no one can identify. Further, in the pages preceding Watt's appearance, Mr Hackett (already identified as a double of Watt) blames his crippled body on a fall off a falling ladder at age one. The insistence on the mothers' negligence during this incident further ties the fall to the birth scene described in the beginning pages of the novel. The burlesque discussion of birth draws particular attention to the severing of the umbilical cord. In other parts of *Watt* as well, birth is termed expulsion or ejection (pp. 104, 216). Moreover, Arsene later compares the cycle of existence — days, seasons, generations of the earth — to vomit, excrement, and a cat's flux, all that flows rejected from the body like a child a birth. Similarly, the threne Watt hears in a ditch just before arriving at Mr Knott's

---

[23] *Samuel Beckett: A Critical Study*, pp. 104-114.

[24] David H. Hesla — *The Shape of Chaos* (Minneapolis: Univ. of Minnesota Press, 1971), p. 63 — links Arsene to Arsenius, a fifth century Christian hermit and saint who, according to Claude Fleury — *Histoire Ecclésiastique*, V (1697) (20 vols.; Paris, 1691-1720), 2 — heard a voice saying to him: "Arsene fuis les hommes, & tu te sauveras." / "Arsene, flee from men, and you will be saved." (My translation.) For a comparison of Arsene with the Preacher of Ecclesiastes, see Richard A. Law, "Mock Evangelism in Beckett's *Watt*," *Modern Language Studies*, 2, No. 2 (1972), 69-72.

speaks of the blooming, drooping, and withering of generations. So that within the progression of Part I of *Watt*, a birth, a fall, Watt's expulsion, the cosmic flux, and the reversed metamorphosis combine to orchestrate the theme of disjunction.

The intriguing picture of dot and circle, broken below, appears particularly linked to these figurations of the experience of disunion. A geometric image of totality, the circle strongly suggests the womb, one of Beckett's preferred images of unity. Accordingly, in a changed position, the painting's impact on Watt diminishes: "And the thought of the point slipping in from below at last, when it came home at last, or to its new home, and the thought of the breach open below perhaps for ever in vain, these thoughts, to please Watt as they did, required the breach to be below, and nowhere else" (p. 130).

It becomes clear that the disunion of things from their origin is an injustice just as it was for Anaximander: "Whence things originated, thither, according to necessity, they must return and perish; for they must pay penalty and be judged for their injustices according to the order of time." Before Beckett, Schopenhauer, sharing Anaximander's point of view, had linked the fall from oneness (that *Watt* stages over and over), which will necessarily lead to death and destruction, to human birth as well as the way of all things.[25] In *Watt*, then, the problematic disjunction is linked both to birth in the first instance and the child's awakening to separateness in the second, as well as to the cosmological antinomies of the Ancients. Part I tells us, for instance, that "if there were two things that Watt disliked, one was the moon, and the other was the sun" (p. 33), and again "if there were two things that Watt loathed, one was the earth, and the other was the sky" (p. 36).

We have seen how Beckett's early prose inscribed a regression toward the unity before the "conflict of flight and flow."[26] "I want

---

[25] The Anaximander quote comes from Friedrich Nietzsche, *Philosophy during the Tragic Age of the Greeks*, Vol. II of *The Complete Works*, trans. Maximilian A. Mügge (1909-1911); rpt. New York: Russell and Russell, 1964), p. 92. Nietzsche connects Anaximander's statement to Schopenhauer's philosophy on pp. 92-93. See also John Burnet, *Early Greek Philosophy*, 4th ed. (1930; rpt. London: Adam and Charles Black, 1963), pp. 8-9 and 52-55.

[26] "Dream," pp. 107-08; quoted in Harvey, p. 326.

very much to be back in the caul, on my back in the dark for ever," is Belacqua's preference.[27] But whereas this precipitated a movement toward death in the works through *Murphy*, *Watt* and the subsequent novels posit an unbornness suggesting the tentative possibility of a yet to be born time of otherness.

Beckett, we learn from the Bair biography, had been much impressed by a statement Jung made during the question and answer period following the talk the writer attented in 1935, the pivotal year when he was writing *Murphy*. During the discussion, Jung said about a little girl whose archetypal dreams seemed to announce the early death she subsequently suffered: "She had never been born entirely."[28] The same year, as we have pointed out, the writer rejected his cultivation of isolation because it negated living. And Murphy is indeed the last of the protagonists to flee, return, flee into death. Subsequently, in *Watt* the unbornness is no longer to be identified with a regressive flight from life but as the regressive/progressive quest for what is yet to be born.

The theme of unbornness is underlined by several entries in *Watt*'s Addenda. Jung's statement is echoed in fragment 16: "never been properly born." The next fragment speaks of "the foetal soul," and finally, number 22 depicts a womblike "soulscape" in which Watt is fixed.

Moving now to the level of Watt's narrative, reiterating his stay at Knott's, we progress from a cosmological to a supernatural discourse, from pre-Socratic to Platonic thought, since Knott's house and garden are the stage of an Augustinian search of the divine within the soul. Within this inner region, where he wishes to come "face to face" with Knott, the icon of the divine, Watt experiences certain movements, the play of forces (p. 117), or an "unintelligible succession of changes" (p. 79). Or more precisely, on this inner stage (which Mallarmé termed "théâtre de notre esprit,

---

[27] "Fingal," in *More Pricks than Kicks*, p. 29.
[28] Jung, *Analytical Psychology*, p. 107. According to Bair (pp. 209-14), Beckett, after hearing Jung's statement, traced his own memories of the womb and of a painful birth as well as the difficult relation to his mother to his incomplete birth. Much later, in conversations in 1961 and 1962 with Lawrence Harvey, Beckett spoke of the intuition of "a presence, embryonic, undeveloped, of a self that might have been but never got born, an être manqué." See *Samuel Beckett: Poet and Critic*, p. 247.

prototype du reste"/"our mind's theatre, the prototype of the rest"),[29] he finds that "a thing that was nothing had happened, with the utmost formal distinctness" (p. 76). Watt, however, finds it necessary to impose a meaning on the anonymous movements he perceives in order "to exorcize" (p. 78); "in self-defence" (p. 79); or to obtain "semantic succour" (p. 83). The entire description then of the Knott domain is but a variation of the *fort/da* game: Watt will try to circumscribe the forces within by trying on them the arsenal of categories inherited from Western thought, to subdue the absence of meaning by the presence of meaning.

Foremost among these categories we find the Logos and numbers through which the Ancients and the Christian Middle Ages thought to explain the cosmos. The Old Testament God created the world by word and "disposed all things by measure and number and weight" (Wisdom 11.20). And in medieval iconography, for instance, God is seated in the center of a circle holding a book (the sign of the Word's creation of the universe out of chaos) or a compass (the sign of the creation of a measurable universe). Consequently, Watt attempts foremost to fit unto the unknown forces the figure of the biblical God, the Logos that mediates and totalizes reality.

Like the ladder in Arsene's statement, the link to totality that has been taken away, Knott stands for the mediator, the knot that will join together broken links. Unlike Murphy, who disdained ladders, Watt hopes Knott will tie him to truth and being, be both mediator and end. Indeed, an Old Testament image of the way to God, the ladder was later identified by medieval writers with Christ, the mediator:

> And since, when anyone lies fallen, he must remain there prostrate unless someone give a helping hand, and he falls in order to rise again [Isaiah, 24, 20], our soul has not been able to be raised perfectly from the things of sense to an intuition of itself and of the eternal Truth in itself unless the Truth, having assumed human form

---

[29] *Crayonné au théâtre*, in *Œuvres complètes* (Paris: Gallimard, 1945), p. 300. (My translation.)

in Christ, should make itself into a ladder, repairing the first ladder which was broken in Adam.[30]

Thus, the text proliferates in teasing comparisons between Knott and the divine Christ, and again between Watt and the dying Christ. Described in biblical language, for instance, Knott recalls the sun: "the few glimpses caught of Mr Knott, by Watt, were not clearly caught, but as it were in a glass, not a looking-glass, a plain glass, an eastern window at morning, a western window at evening" (p. 147). Whereas Watt's fallen, loaded-down existence, which calls down upon him the attacks of others, brings to mind a different image of Christ.[31] Although for a fleeting moment, the

---

[30] Saint Bonaventura, *The Mind's Road to God*, trans. George Boas (New York: Liberal Arts Press, 1953), p. 28. Nor does it come as a surprise that Saint Bonaventura is mentioned on page 29 of *Watt* in a passage mocking theological absurdities. David H. Hesla — *The Shape of Chaos*, p. 12 — indicates that the image of the ladder in the heart appears in Psalms 84.5, in Saint Augustine (*Confessions* 13.9), in St. John Climacus *(The Ladder of Divine Ascent)*, and in William Butler Yeats ("The Circus Animals' Desertion"). On p. 13 f. and p. 64 f., Hesla further links the image of the ladder in the mind to Descartes (*Rules for the Direction of the Mind*, Rule V), Hegel (Preface to *Phenomenology of the Spirit*), and Kierkegaard *(Johannes Climacus)*. Many critics have taken up Jacqueline Hoefer's identification of the ladder as Wittgenstein's "ladder of logic" whose inadequacy the novel shows. See her article *"Watt," Perspective*, 11 (Autumn 1959), 166-82; rpt. in *Samuel Beckett: A Collection of Critical Essays*, ed. Martin Esslin (Englewood Cliffs, N.J.: Prentice-Hall, 1965), pp. 62-76. In "Fritz Mauthner's 'Critique of Language' in Samuel Beckett's *Watt*," *Contemporary Literature*, 15 (1974), 474-87, Jennie Skerl, refuting Hoefer's article, replaces Wittgenstein with Mauthner as the philosopher whose theories on language *Watt* illustrates. Skerl (p. 477) quotes from Mauthner — *Beiträge zu einer Kritik der Sprache*, 1st ed. (Stuttgart: Cotta, 1901), I, 2; trans. Gershon Weiler, "On Fritz Mauthner's *Critique of Language*," *Mind*, 67 (1958), 80 — and suggests another model for the ladder: "Finally, the highest degree of critical attitude, according to Mauthner, is silence, and this is where the critique of language leads, like a ladder: 'If I want to ascend into the critique of language, which is the most important business of thinking mankind, then I must destroy language behind me and in me, step by step: I must destroy every rung of the ladder while climbing upon it.'" Skerl (p. 483, n. 16) also mentions that the ladder in *Watt* might allude to Tim Finnegan's fall from a ladder in *Finnegans Wake*. What most critics would agree upon, then, is that, within the context of Arsene's prophetic statement, the ladder that has been removed stands in one way or another for the Logos.

[31] The similarities between Watt's journey and the Stations of the Cross were first discussed by David H. Hesla, in "The Shape of Chaos:

two Christ-like images, Knott and Watt, suggest a unity in the garden (p. 146) — like Arsene and the sun in the yard, like Sam and Watt in one garden — Watt-*pharmakon* does not reconnect with a divine Knott.

Moreover, Knott's grotesque physicality contradicts the transcendence of the figure: the arrangement of his furniture, his clothing, his meals, his physical appearance are described in lengthy lists detailing probable combinations and finally claiming no connection with what they are meant to describe. For, secondly, the power of the Logos is contradicted by Watt's fall outside the symbolic order: words, once tied to what they named, have become disjointed from their objects just as numbers have no relation to reality. So that in the absence of the ladder of Logos, incidents (the arrival of the Galls, for example), outer and inner reality (the pot and Watt and Knott) become unnamable, indecipherable. The failing power of the Logos is further underscored by the theme of impotency which Watt's relation to the fishwoman and the "Bando" discussion amply and comically develop.[32]

Finally then, Watt admits that the unnamable forces at play cannot be covered by the traditional figures of the divine. There is no mediator, no logos, no number to replace the absent ladder to the circle of being, or the "being of nothing" (p. 39). Watt speaks of the failure of his quest in Augustinian terms:

> Of nought. To the source. To the teacher. To the temple. To him I brought. This emptied heart. These emptied hands. This mind ignoring. This body homeless.... Abandoned my little to find him. (p. 166)[33]

A Reading of Beckett's *Watt*," *Critique: Studies in Modern Fiction*, 6 (Spring 1963), 88-89.

[32] In this connection one is reminded of what Jacques Derrida attacks under the general heading of Western Philosophy's *phallogocentrisme*. On the status of language in *Watt*, see particularly Olga Bernal, *Language et fiction dans le roman de Beckett;* Jennie Skerl, "Fritz Mauthner's 'Critique of Language' in Samuel Beckett's *Watt;*" and Linda Ben-Zvi, "Samuel Beckett, Fritz Mauthner, and the Limits of Language," *PMLA*, 95 (1980), 183-200.

[33] This quote is an example of Watt's inversion of the sentences in a group.

The "emptied heart" quite obviously refers to Augustine's unquiet heart in the *Confessions* 1.1.: "our heart is restless until it rests in you," to which Beckett had already alluded in the final lines of "Sanies I," the sixth poem of *Echo's Bones:* "and let the tiger go on smiling/in our hearts that funds ways home." Fragment 23 of the Addenda adds to the images of the empty heart and hands and of the "dim" and then "dark" mind's road that of a flame "going out/gone out." Similarly, in the *Confessions* 13.9, Augustine alternates the imagery of the steps in the heart with that of an inward fire enkindled by God. In "The Addenda to Samuel Beckett's *Watt*," moreover, Rubin Rabinovitz notes that the image of a flame about to go out helps to explain the game Watt plays with the dying coals on entering Knott's house.[34]

Throughout, Watt encounters instead of a divine presence, a ladder that has been removed, a dark mind, an empty heart, an extinguished fire in the soul. His is a word without grace. The game of come and go with the mystic presence within the soul remains suspended like all the other versions of the game in *Watt*.

Nor can the divine logos be replaced by a human one; no human name can satisfy Watt's semantic need:

> And Watt's need of semantic succour was at times so great that he would set to trying names on things, and on himself, almost as a woman hats.... As for himself, though he could no longer call it a man, as he had used to do, with the intuition that he was perhaps not talking nonsense, yet he could not imagine what else to call it, if not a man. (p. 83)

Instead of coming face to face with an image of self, Watt experiences an otherness so radical that is must remain unnamed.

As discussed earlier, on the next narrative level, where Sam meets Watt in the asylum garden, the Cartesian search for self-presence in the mind just as the omniscient level's empirical circumscriptions similarly come to nothing, nothing yet.[35] The natural

---

[34] In *Samuel Beckett: The Art of Rhetoric*, ed. Edouard Morot-Sir, et al. (Chapel Hill: North Carolina Studies in the Romance Languages and Literatures, 1976), p. 212.

[35] The Sam/Watt duality, with Sam's rational search and Watt's mystical quest, is analogous to the distinction between two selves made in

or cosmic, the supernatural or divine, both immanent and transcendent, the human — rational or empirical, linguistic or non-linguistic — ways to truth are but so many games the mind plays with itself, its *fort/da* game with light and dark.

It becomes clear, however, that the quests for totality linked to cosmic, divine, and anthropomorphic oppositions are not innocent games, for they lead to violence. Indeed, *Watt* stages a ferocious attack on the anthropomorphic concept of divinity. Thus, certain painfully cruel scenes in the novel link human violence to the divine. In Part I, Lady McCann throws a stone at Watt: "And it is to be supposed that God, always favourable to the McCanns of?, guided her hand, for the stone fell on Watt's hat and struck it from his head, to the ground" (p. 32). The reference to God's part in the violence and the play on the name Mary, make this episode especially fierce. In Part IV, the bucket ("I declare to God she sprang out of me hands, like as if she was alive, said Mr. Nolan" [p. 241].) succeeds in knocking down and bloodying Watt.[36] These scenes in the omniscient frame narrative are reinforced on the next level by Watt as Sam's mirror image: "His face was bloody, his hands also, and thorns were in his scalp" (p. 159).

This imitation of Christ is doubled by an imitation of the violent God, for Sam and Watt in their little garden would delight in destroying birds and particularly "larks' nests, laden with eggs still warm from the mother's breast" (p. 155), or in taking a young rat confidently resting in their bosom and feeding it to its mother or father or other relative, such actions making them feel "nearest to God" (p. 156). The projection of their own weakness (the *pharmakon* the inner glass mirrors to them) onto scapegoats (the animals in the garden) is doubled by an introjection of cruelty leading to an unending cycle of violence. (Like Murphy's zone of

---

mystical psychology, between *Animus,* a surface self concerned with rational knowledge, and *Anima,* the deep self turned toward mystical or poetic knowledge. The voices speaking within Watt are similarly related to the experience of many mystics. The analogy is incomplete, however, since the novel obviously mocks the mystic as well as the rational paths.

[36] Richard A. Law ("Mock Evangelism in Beckett's *Watt,*" pp. 78-79) finds that the Resurrection of Christ is parodied in the train station scene of Part IV and that further allusions suggest that Watt is a ritualistic scapegoat.

revenge, this terror in the psyche is an "interior" reduplication of the violence raging outside.) Sam/Watt are the victims of a cruel God, with whom they identify as they in turn massacre and kill. René Girard, who postulates that the scapegoat mechanism is at the origin of all cultures, points out in recent works that it is this projection of hostility onto the divine that has served to camouflage and intensify human violence in history.[37]

Beckett's subsequent novels, exploring the ways in which the identification with a cruel divinity is related to paternal and maternal imprints and the double bind of the *fort/da* game, will aim at dismantling these violent projections. (That Western religions of the Judaeo-Christian-Islamic tradition, which identify God with The Father beyond whom none can aim, maintain their faithful in an infantile state has been pointed out by Joseph Campbell.)[38] It now becomes understandable why the divine figures of tradition, evoked in anthropomorphic and mythic terms, both female and male, through the immanence of the womb-earthmother (the union in the garden) or the transcendence of the sun-father, through the circle of the *Ewig-Weibliche* or the Logos, are so ferociously ridiculed in Beckett's works: "And if there were two things that Watt loathed, one was the earth, and the other was the sky" (p. 36). It would seem that these old images block the process that seeks to give birth to the otherness of non-violent times.

---

[37] See *La Violence et le sacré* (Paris: Grasset, 1972), trans. as *Violence and the Sacred* (Baltimore: Johns Hopkins Univ. Press, 1977); and *Des choses cachées depuis la fondation du monde* (Paris: Grasset, 1978). In the latter work, Girard argues that a non-sacrificial reading of the New Testament, a deconstruction of the concept of divine violence, is required to help break the pattern of reciprocal human violence.

[38] See "Bios and Mythos: Prolegomena to a Science of Mythology," in *Psychoanalysis and Culture*, eds. G. B. Wilbur and M. Muensterberger (New York: International Universities Press, 1951); rpt. in *Myth and Literature*, ed. John B. Vickery (Lincoln: Univ. of Nebraska Press, 1966), p. 22.

It is interesting to note as well that in 1935, in his fifth Tavistock lecture, Jung (*Analytical Psychology*, pp. 181-85) had theorized that Hitlerism and Fascism were religious phenomena activated by the projection of an archetypal savior image. As we have seen, *Watt* repeatedly holds this image up to ridicule.

In general, *En attendant Godot,* written a few years later, plays with the same categories as *Watt.* Godot, like Knott, represents the attempt to call onto the stage the absent (off-stage) forces. And as in *Watt,* the play devalues the traditional images:

> VLADIMIR.—Il a une barbe, Monsieur Godot? / (softly) Has he a beard, Mr. Godot?
> GARÇON/BOY.—Oui Monsieur. / Yes Sir.
> VLADIMIR.—Blonde ou... *(il hésite)...* ou noire? / Fair or... *(he hesitates)...* or black?
> GARÇON/BOY *(hésitant).*—Je crois qu'elle est blanche, Monsieur. / I think it's white, Sir.
>
> *Silence.*
>
> VLADIMIR.—Miséricorde. / Christ have mercy on us! (p. 159 / p. 59)

The hesitations and Vladimir's exclamation suggest that if Godot is identified with the old father-image, there is no hope.

In the play, the image of the absent ladder or knot is turned into a play on the word *lier* (to be tied); there is no re-ligion yet:

> ESTRAGON *(mâche, avale).*—Je demande si on est lié. / *(chews, swallows).* I'm asking you if we're tied.
> VLADIMIR.—Lié? / Tied?
> ESTRAGON.—Lié. / Tied.
> VLADIMIR.—Comment lié? / How do you mean tied?
> ESTRAGON.—Pieds et poings. / Down.
> VLADIMIR.—Mais à qui? Par qui? / But to whom? By whom?
> ESTRAGON.—A ton bonhomme. / To your man.
> VLADIMIR.—A Godot? Lié à Godot? Quelle idée! Jamais de la vie! *(Un temps.)* Pas encore. *(Il ne fait pas la liaison.)* / To Godot? Tied to Godot! What an idea! No question of it. *(Pause.)* For the moment. (p. 32 / p. 14)

Immediately after this exchange, Pozzo and Lucky, tied to each other by a rope, caricature the old type of union, like Knott and Watt, of master and servant. Consequently, in both acts, Estragon first mistakes the tyrannical Pozzo for Godot, an identification accepted by some critics.[39] Instead, of course, Pozzo and Lucky represent the known fraternity of violence, whereas Vladimir and Estragon, tied neither to Godot, themselves, nor nothingness (they lack a rope with which to hang themselves) share Watt's namelessness (their names change throughout the play), and his fallen, disjointed state. Like Watt they try on hats and shoes, play with empty words.

The mythic images of earth and sky resurface in the subsequent texts up through the cylinder-world of *Le Dépeupleur* (1970) / *The Lost Ones* (in which ladders reappear as well):

> De tout temps le bruit court ou encore mieux l'idée a cours qu'il existe une issue.... Pour les uns il ne peut s'agir que d'un passage dérobé prenant naissance dans un des tunnels et menant comme dit le poète aux asiles de la nature. Les autres rêvant d'une trappe dissimulée au centre du plafond donnant accès à une cheminée au bout de laquelle brilleraient encore le soleil et les autres étoiles. (pp. 16-17)

> From time immemorial rumour has it or better still the notion is abroad that there exists a way out.... One school swears by a secret passage branching from one of the tunnels and leading in the words of the poet to nature's sanctuaries. The other dreams of a trapdoor hidden in the hub of the ceiling giving access to a flue at the end of which the sun and other stars would still be shining. (pp. 17-18)

Strikingly, the most important elements of the cylinder's order are not the faulty ladders and tunnels, but the particular images that preside over the quest. For were the inhabitants of the cylinder-world willing to cooperate in setting up a vertical ladder, success would be within reach. However, again, the very efforts to reach the exits under the controlling myths of immanence and transcendence (here related to Romantic poetry's nature mysticism and the *Divine Comedy*'s final vision) reduce relationships between searchers to solitude or violence:

---

[39] Among others, C. Chadwick holds this view. See his "*Waiting for Godot*: A Logical Approach," *Symposium*, 14 (Winter 1960), 252-57.

> Un moment de fraternité. Mais celle-ci en dehors des flambées de violence leur est aussi étrangère qu'aux papillons. Ce n'est pas tant par manque de cœur ou d'intelligence qu'à cause de l'idéal dont chacun est la proie. Voilà pour ce zénith inviolable où se cache aux yeux des amateurs de mythe une issue vers terre et ciel. (p. 19)
>
> An instant of fraternity. But outside their explosions of violence this sentiment is as foreign to them as to butterflies. And this owing not so much to want of heart or intelligence as to the ideal preying on one and all. So much for this inviolable zenith where for amateurs of myth lies hidden a way out to earth and sky. (p. 21)

Nostalgia for the old myths resurfaces and is rejected. In *Mercier et Camier,* written shortly after *Watt,* we read: "Finalement il se dit, Je suis Mercier, seul, malade, dans le froid, dans l'humidité, vieux, à moitié fou, empêtré dans une histoire sans issue. Il regarda un instant, avec nostalgie, le ciel hideux, la terre affreuse. A ton âge, se dit-il" (p. 101)./"In the end he said, I am Mercier, alone, ill, in the cold, the wet, old, half mad, no way on, no way back. He eyed briefly, with nostalgia, the ghastly sky, the hideous earth. At your age, he said" (p. 62).

It is the two parts of *Molloy,* however, which most insistently and maliciously dismantle the old myths linked to earth and sky, the immanence of mother divinities, the transcendence of father gods. We have seen that Molloy and Moran are two opposing and complementary parts of one persona. Their journeys, best told in the mythological present, each lasting a double turn of seasons, each suggesting a regressive/progressive movement toward an unborn state, are but one journey staged at different psychic levels. The multiple narrative levels, which were linked to the archeology of philosophical thought in *Watt* as well as to different layers of the mind — sense perception, rational thought, mystic experience — in *Molloy,* are associated with a psychoanalytic topology. To see how, we must reexamine the implications of the *fort/da* game which structures the text.

A recent book, applying a semiotic model to psychoanalytic theory, analyzes this game as an instance of a triple mirror symmetrical inversion.[40] Basing their analysis of repression on Melanie Klein's theory, the authors describe how during the process of repression, painful perceptions are kept below the level of consciousness by a refusal to verbalize them. However, an inverted version of the painful perception is verbalized, thus transforming what is unpleasurable into what is pleasurable. In this manner, a double code is generated in relation to the desirable and undesirable positions. In the case of the child's game with the wooden reel, the child has to accept his being abandoned or expelled (from the maternal presence) or risk the displeasure of his mother. He therefore refuses to see the unpleasant reality of his role (being expelled) by repressing it and then projecting it onto the toy: the toy is what is expelled. At the same time, he denies, refuses to see the role of expeller that his mother holds in relation to him: instead, he introjects this position; he is the expeller. He thus represses what is painful (being exiled) and adopts it inverted pleasurable form (exiling).

The relation between these inverted positions in the game can be schematized as follows:[41]

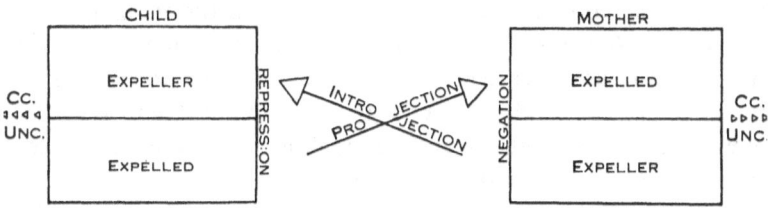

The child, refusing to see what is painful in himself, projects the expelled role onto the toy he substituted for his mother. And disdaining to see what is a pleasurable role in the other, he adopts the expelling posture. Thus the child's game inverts the positions at work in reality by means of a triple mirror inversion. A narcis-

---

[40] Maria Carmen Gear and Ernesto Liendo, in collaboration with Luis J. Prieto, *Sémiologie psychanalytique*, trans. from the Spanish by Marie Tulien and Daniel Glauser (Paris: Minuit, 1975), pp. 282-85 ff. See also Eugen S. Bär's review article on the above book, "Semiotic Model Theory in Psychoanalysis," *Semiotica*, 26, No. 1/2 (1979), 99-119.

[41] This schema is adapted from Gear and Liendo, p. 284, fig. 45, which illustrates the Dora-Freud interaction.

sistic mirror effects an inverted perception, that is, the expelled sees himself as expeller. The child thus gives himself the active role, although his playing is a way of accepting his passive state. Through his game he seems to say, "I'm expelling you," but says in fact, "I permit you to expel me," constituting a semantic mirror of inverted speech. And finally, these two mirrors are joined by a third, the oedipal mirror of sexual inversion.

Gear and Liendo (op. cit., p. 286) point out that in the case of the little boy with the reel, the mother plays an ambivalent role, for she transmits contradictory commands, "love me / don't love me." The two psychoanalysts find that such conflicting instructions (do/don't), related to an inner instinctual necessity, produce a pragmatically paradoxical superego when interiorized. This agency emits verbal orders (on the moral plane) and simultaneously nonverbal instructions (on the experiential plane) that contradict each other and put the child into a double bind.[42]

The situation of a male child within the oedipal configuration is consequently as follows. The father produces the verbal message (a conscious moral order), "do as I do, be like me (or else you are not a man)," and the nonverbal message (an unconscious command), "don't do as I do (take my place with the mother), don't be like me (or else I'll emasculate you)." The mother's verbal message, on the other hand, commands the child to be like her in order to avoid the father's threat, whereas her nonverbal demand asks him to be a man like his father. This double semiotic paradox may be schematized as follows:

	FATHER	MOTHER	
VERBAL	BE YOUR FATHER [FATHER POSITION]	BE YOUR MOTHER [MOTHER POSITION]	MODEL (GOOD)
NONVERBAL	DON'T BE YOUR FATHER (BE YOUR MOTHER) [MOTHER' POSITION]	DON'T BE YOUR MOTHER (BE YOUR FATHER) [FATHER' POSITION]	RIVAL (BAD)

---

[42] Gear and Liendo refer to Gregory Batenson's theory of the double bind on p. 289 ff. See the latter's "Toward a Theory of Schizophrenia," in *Ecology of Mind*, pp. 201-27.

THEMATIC REDUPLICATION

The child, faced with these two sets of communicational paradoxes, reacts with the double alibi (in accordance with the *fort/da* strategy), "I say that I am my father, but I am actually my mother," thus alternately covering the contradictory demands.[43] By introjection, he assumes the identity of father (the Father' position) and ignores his actual identity with the mother (Mother') which he projects on others:

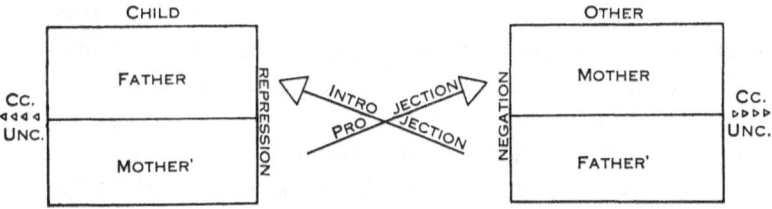

Yet, just as with the expeller/expelled duality, by saying that he is his father, he is actually accepting his difference from the father. He is split into two, just as the mother and father figures are each divided into good/bad, model/rival.

If we now examine how the *fort/da* game functions in *Molloy*, we will find that it is the three mirror inversions which produce the symmetries and asymmetries of the multi-layered text. Molloy (the persona), who is just the opposite of Moran, as we have seen, perceives himself alternately as A and B, but most consistently identifies with the maternal figure. Indeed, for Molloy, the mother-figure is all encompassing. She is the origin of life and therefore of death and the one who sustains him (she gives him money). He hates her for expelling him — birth is described as anal expulsion (p. 22 / p. 16) — and is always on his way back to her. Molloy thus variously describes her as his sexless, undifferentiated equal (p. 23 / p. 17), that is, his other self, or he merges her with Ruth-Rose (Eros), his one experience with love (p. 89 / p. 59), and with Loy-Lousse, a representation of the law and an obstacle on

---

[43] Gear and Liendo, pp. 324-28.

his way. Finally, the three maternal figures, Mag, Rose, Loy, blending into one another, are identified with the image of the old hag, an androgynous, monstrous sphinx: "je suis tenté de n'y voir qu'une seule et même vioque, aplatie et enragée par la vie" (p. 89). / "I am tempted to think of them as one and the same old hag, flattened and crazed by life" (p. 59). Mag (suggesting a blend of "Ma" and "hag") thus is both mother and not mother, self and other, model and rival, good and bad, desired and hated, goal and obstacle.

At the beginning of this version of what Molloy terms an "irréel voyage" (p. 22) / "unreal journey" (p. 16), the single-minded resolve to go to his mother is likened to child's play: "ce fut pour moi un jeu d'enfant, d'enfant unique, de m'en remplir l'esprit, jusqu'à ce que toute autre préoccupation en fût bannie" (p. 21. / "it was child's play for me, the play of an only child, to fill my mind until it was rid of all other preoccupations" (p. 15).

His resolve is further bolstered, the reader learns later, by an inner voice, the famous "hypothetical imperative" that both sets Molloy on the way to his mother and then falls silent: "Et dans cet ordre qui hésitait, puis mourait, comment ne pas sous-entendre, Molloy, n'en fais rien!" (pp. 133-34) / "And in this command which faltered, then died, it was hard not to hear the unspoken entreaty, Don't do it, Molloy" (p. 87). The voice, then, verbally orders Molloy to do what it nonverbally commands him not to do, placing him in a double bind. The ambiguous command, however, does no more than strengthen and then mock his innate desire, which like the voice is divided against itself: "Heureusement qu'en somme il ne faisait qu'appuyer, pour ridiculiser par la suite si l'on veut, une disposition permanente et qui n'avait pas besoin d'apostrophes pour se savoir velléitaire. Et tout seul, et depuis toujours, j'allais vers ma mère..." (p. 134). / "Fortunately it did no more than stress, the better to mock if you like, an innate velleity. And of myself, all my life, I think I had been going to my mother..." (p. 87). Going to his mother is thus an original desire which is divided between the forces of life and death, and which the good/bad mother and the introjected communicational paradoxes of the superego reinforce.

Molloy's narrative throughout sounds echoes from the Oedipus story to the extent that it can be read as one version of the myth. Molloy's father is mentioned only once when Molloy voices the suspicion that his mother takes him for his father: "Moi je la prenais pour ma mère et elle elle me prenait pour mon père" (p. 23). / "I took her for my mother and she took me for my father" (p. 17). He is both the son who identifies with the mother and the son identified with the father. Accordingly, Mag's name for Molloy is Dan, blending "Da," meaning "father" in his region, the narrator specifies, with "son." Thus, the mother would have the son be the father (not castrated) whereas the father intimates castration for this position. As a result, Molloy meets with obstacles that threaten him and block his path, that is, various personifications of a phallocentric law, the policeman, the sergeant who menaces him with a cylindrical ruler while demanding to know his identity, and the charcoal burner. The father's law, however, is no less ambiguous than the mother's for it paradoxically stops Molloy from continuing on his way and then lets him go on. Thus Molloy is partly relieved to be arrested — "Oublieux de ma mère, libéré des actes, fondu dans l'heure des autres, me disant répit, répit" (pp. 29-30) / "Forgetful of my mother, set free from the act, merged in this alien hour, saying, Respite, respite" (p. 21) — and fails to understand why the sergeant frees him: "je m'étonnais de retrouver si vite la liberté, si c'était bien elle, et sans qu'il fût question de la moindre sanction" (p. 34). / "I was surprised to find myself so soon at freedom once again, if that is what it was, unpenalised" (p. 24). Here, then, the inner maternal imperative's "do/don't, go/don't go" is inverted to the paternal "don't/do, don't go/go," the double oedipal paradox. As a consequence, the text in several instances identifies Molloy with a victim of the law. [44]

---

[44] In *Mercier et Camier*, the same motifs appear, combined as intriguingly if less effectively. Just as the policeman accuses Molloy for his way of resting, so a ranger forces Mercier and Camier to leave their shelter while calling them assassins. Once on their way, a voice whispers to them, "Le sac! Votre sac!" (p. 95)/"The sack! Your sack!" (p. 60). They have the intuition that the sack contains objects "indispensables à notre salut" (p. 94)/"essential to our salvation" (p. 59) and is "le noeud de toute cette affaire" (p. 93-94)/"the crux of the whole matter" (p. 59) and, at the same time, claim to know that this is not so. The sack here takes on the containing/contained relation of the womb, of the original relation to the mother which Mercier and Camier think is and is not essential. In any

Molloy's crippled legs and his violent encounter with the charcoal burner in the forest further parallel the Oedipus myth. Before meeting the man, the narrator indicates that "de temps en temps je tombais sur une sorte de carrefour" (p. 127) / "from time to time I came on a kind of crossroads" (p. 83), announcing the fatal crossroads of the myth. At first, the charcoal-burner arouses Molloy's filial love: "J'aurais pu l'aimer, je crois, si j'avais eu soixante-dix ans de moins" (p. 128). / "I might have loved him, I think, if I had been seventy years younger" (p. 83). However, when Molloy asks the way to the nearest city (where he hopes to find his mother), he fails to understand the man's reply. This misunderstanding found in all the encounters with paternal figures, added to the man's attempt to stop his progress, perhaps with the intent to keep him near himself, brings Molloy to the fatal violence described as a deliberate, methodical repetition of Oedipus' flash of anger against the stranger barring his way.

Within Molloy's narrative, the external obstacles to his mother-quest are the various father personifications of the law, that first forbid then stop forbidding. To these must be added the internal obstacles, the introjected law of the mother, that both demands then stops demanding. Finally, of course, Molloy fails to reach his destination, for he ends in a ditch awaiting transfer to the maternal room. Once he reaches the room, however, as we know from the preamble, instead of finding his mother, he takes her place. Was his then a journey to life or death? The ditch and the room suggest the tomb and the womb, leaving Molloy simultaneously dead and unborn. His journey has both regressed and progressed to the womb/tomb mother. In accordance with the *fort/da*'s inverted mirror strategy, then, Molloy (the expelled) sees himself as his mother, identifies with the bad mother's inverted image, is

---

case, it is their duty to find the sack. During their search, when Mercier and Camier come to the "rue fatale" (p. 164)/"fatal alley" (p. 96) and ask a policeman the way to a house of prostitution, he tries to stop them until they kill him. Thus, the law forces them on their way (the first policeman) and is an obstacle on their way (the second policeman who is killed). A further allusion to the Oedipus myth appears in the latter policeman's number: "Seize cent soixante-cinq, dit Camier. L'année de la pestilence" (p. 156). / "Sixteen sixty-five, said Camier. The year of the plague" (p. 92).

finally reabsorbed in the mother, thus avoiding both life and death for the double alibi of an unborn state.

The discussion of the lengthy Lousse episode (roughly one-third of Molloy's part) has been purposely set aside until this point, for in it Molloy's narrative redoubles itself within itself. By means of this centrally placed *mise en abyme,* Molloy's narrative, staging a descent into the psyche, proceeds into a further *descente en enfer.* In Jungian terms, which seem appropriate here, Lousse's closed-off garden represents the innermost region of the psyche, the mother's realm, in which the complex figure of Sophie Loy-Lousse takes on all possible maternal roles, both positive and negative.

Before entering her garden, by killing Teddy, Lousse's dog, Molloy reenacts Oedipus' encounter with the sphinx. Some mythic theories identify the sphinx with a divine totemic animal and see in its killing a repetiton of the death of the father: "Oedipus has not only slain his father, but in his father he has struck at the supreme authority, the God himself." [45] The way Teddy's death is staged and his name ("Theodore" cointains the Greek for "gift" and "god"; in English, of course, "dog" is the anagram of "god") suggest the archaic death of the father-god. [46] Teddy's death causes Molloy to fall off the bicycle (a dynamic replacement of Watt's ladder) and to enter the paradisiacal garden of the mother.

Like Oedipus, then, and in an archetypal repetition of the Mag-Dan relation, Molloy identifies with the father-god since he twice repeats that Teddy's grave is his own, and he is asked to take the father's place: "Je remplacerais en quelque sorte le chien que j'avais tué et qui lui tenait lieu d'enfant" (p. 70). / "I would as it were take the place of the dog I had killed, as it for her had taken the place of a child" (p. 47). At the same time, in line with the double bind paradox, Molloy identifies with the mother figure, since on awakening at the house of Lousse, he finds himself dressed in a woman's nightgown, shaven of his beard, perfumed with lavender, oblivious of who he is. He describes the moon at length and later his merging with the garden, with the whole cosmos, in

---

[45] Theodor Reik, *Dogma and Compulsion: Psychoanalytic Studies of Religion and Myths,* trans. Bernard Miall (New York: International Universities Press, 1951), p. 328.

[46] This episode brings to mind *Godot*'s familiar round song which features the death and burial of a dog.

an experience of immanence: "Et il y avait un autre bruit, celui de ma vie qui faisait sienne ce jardin chevauchant la terre des abîmes et des déserts" (p. 73). "And there was another noise, that of my life become the life of this garden as it rode the earth of deeps and wildernesses" (p. 49).

In Lousse's garden, then, Molloy has reached the stage of immanence in the universal mother. Lousse combines not only the three fundamental images of the mother, the oedipal mother (she asks Molloy to take the place of Teddy), the oral mother who nourishes (she feeds Molloy), the primitive uterine mother (in her garden Molloy experiences the mythic return to the womb of the earth-mother), but she suggests a cluster of archetypal mother goddesses, particularly the triple-bodied Hecate. In *Symbols of Transformation,* the first version of which was published in 1912, Jung lists the following attributes (among others) of this divinity, all of which find echoes in the Lousse episode: Hecate is a chthonian mother goddess of death and rebirth, the guardian of the gates of Hades, a goddess of night who sends moonsickness, the mother of witchcraft and witches. She is confused with Artemis, the huntress with hounds, with Aphrodite, with Persephone, and Rhea, the All-Mother. One of Hecate's symbols is the dagger, and she is shown on a gnostic gem with a cross on her head. At crossroads, which were dedicated to her, dog-sacrifices were offered to her. The crossing, Jung specifies, signifies both union and parting, the dual relation to the mother.[47] (The x-shaped knife-rest Molloy steals from Lousse again comes to mind as the emblem of a mythic complex.)

Most importantly, though, Hecate is also a figure of the bad mother whom Jung identified with the sphinx: "The Sphinx is a semi-theriomorphic representation of the mother-imago, or rather of the Terrible Mother, who has left numerous traces in mythology."[48] Marie Delcourt's version of the sphinx similarly insists on an archaic female monster intent on attacking and raping young men, an image that Lévi-Strauss links to the "old hag" of native North American and Celtic myths. In the Celtic myth, if the

---

[47] *Symbols of Transformation,* 2nd ed., trans. R. F. C. Hull (Princeton: Princeton Univ. Press, 1967), pp. 369-71.

[48] *Symbols of Transformation,* p. 179.

young hero responds to the advances of the old hag, she is transformed into a young woman who helps him to acceed to power.[49] It is striking that this version appears in Beckett's 1962 radio play, *Words and Music*, where the old hag or sphinx dissolves into a beautiful woman in whose eyes lies the answer to life's enigma. The first version of the old hag ("Age is when to a man / Huddled o'er the ingle / Shivering for the hag / To put the pan in the bed") fades into the face in the ashes of a woman, sensually evoked. Within the eyes of this face, called back from the past, may be glimpsed beyond self-reflection the source of life: "Then down a little way / Through the trash ... To whence one glimpse / Of that wellhead."[50]

Molloy, of course, reduces all the female figures, repulsive Mag, ambiguous Lousse, Ruth-Rose, who attacked him on a garbage dump and with whom he copulated like a dog, to an old hag of uncertain sex. Consequently, in the Lousse episode, the sphinx, both the bad father and the terrible mother, is dual like all the other figures. Lousse's sorcery — her poisoning of Molloy's food and drink recall Hecate and, as many have seen, Circe — her haglike appearance and her role as obstacle all bring to mind the terrible mother version of the sphinx. And indeed Molloy, unable to decide whether Lousse is male, female, or androgynous asks himself: "Une femme aurait-elle pu m'arrêter dans mon élan vers ma mère? Sans doute" (p. 85). / "Could a woman have stopped me as I swept towards mother? Probably" (p. 56). Like Mag, Lousse is both mother and hag, positive and negative, good and bad.

As a personification of the paradoxical law (Loy), Lousse is the ruler of a matricentric realm (all the servants are male) in which she holds Molloy captive, but does nothing to prevent his escape. Further mythic echoes and plays on her names make Sophie Lousse, on the one hand, Sophia, divine wisdom and keeper of

---

[49] In "La Structure des mythes," in *Anthropologie structurale* (Paris: Plon, 1958), p. 238, n. 1, Claude Lévi-Strauss refers to Marie Delcourt's *Oedipe ou la légende du conquérant* (Liège, 1944) and briefly discusses the various versions of the sphinx. The article by Lévi-Strauss appeared originally as "The Structural Study of Myth," *Journal of American Folklore*, 78, No. 270 (1955), pp. 428-44.

[50] *"Cascando" and Other Short Dramatic Pieces* (New York: Grove Press, 1968?), pp. 28; 31-32.

the garden of Dante's Earthly Paradise. (Her sowing of multi-colored flowers evokes the Paradise's Matilda.) On the other hand, that Lousse is Lucifer is hinted not only by the play on sounds but by her intention to have old Teddy put to death, her revolt against the father god. Thus, if Lousse's garden is paradise, the innermost region of the psyche, it is also a hellish prison from which Molloy must and does escape. For although he has reached the mythic oneness with the mother, the negative Nirvana of a return to the womb no longer satisfies the quest which spirals on, leaving an unanswered riddle, an unborn hero.

From an examination of the incidents of Molloy's narrative, then, it appears that the components of the Oedipus myth are inscribed in duplicate. The Lousse episode condenses the entire drama into a dream-like emblem in the middle of the narrative which, since it stages embedded inner journeys to the mother, traces Molloy's movements through regions that evoke the mother and the unconscious: the walled city of his birth, the seashore, the dark forest, and the central garden of Lousse. The quest, as we have seen, is both commanded and forbidden by multiple embodiments of a paradoxical law: maternal voices that order and forbid, paternal figures that obstruct and goad, sphinxes both male and female. The violence against the father, of which there are two versions, and the union with the mother figures, however, fail to lead anywhere. Indeed, rather than Oedipus, Molloy is an anti-Oedipus, for instead of solving the riddle of the sphinx and attaining sovereignty, Molloy in a regressive movement recedes from the mother's room via the sphinx to the killing of the stranger at the crossroads to the final crawling on all fours out of the forest into the bowels of the earth.

As in *Watt,* the mythic, religious, literary, and philosophical texts that *Molloy* quotes directly or indirectly are first fractured into echoing fragments and ultimately discarded. Thus, the two versions of the Oedipus myth intertwine with the journeys of Dionysos, Ulysses, Hermes, Christ, and Dante, all of which include a descent into hell. In addition to the Lousse-Circe-Calypso figure, there are echoes of the Ulysses story in the Hermes-like valet in sandals (pp. 64-65 / p. 43), in the brief appearance of the Sirens (p. 29 / p. 21), of Nausicaa on the seashore (p. 114 / p. 75), and of the boat of Ulysses (p. 76 / p. 51). The allusions to Christ are extended by comparing Molloy's journey to an endless flight into an Egypt of exile (p. 100 / p. 66), to a hopeless calvary (p. 120 / p. 78) and by identifying him with a sacrificial victim (pp. 38, 41, 57 / pp. 27, 28, 38). Dante's Purgatory is evoked at the beginning and at the end of Part I together with a descent into hell and an ascent to the Earthly Paradise. In *Molloy*, however, each of these journeys is deprived of its goal: Molloy-Ulysses is without a homeland — "Qui, ne m'éloignant de nulle patrie, ne m'emporte vers nul naufrage" (p. 76). / "Which, as it bears me from no fatherland away, bears me onward to no shipwreck" (p. 51) — Molloy-Christ without salvation; Molloy-Dante without paradise; Molloy-Oedipus without a mother, for as we know from the preamble, Molloy not finding her, replaces her. And since, as we have seen, all of Molloy's narrative is dictated by a disturbance of the silence within, by murmurs which he calls lies, the mythic echoes of the past are ultimately rejected for a voice whose language is yet to be deciphered. *Molloy*, embedding its intriguing versions of the old myths within this negating matatextual frame, thus dismantles the mythic and other theoretical categories which have been applied through time to the basic antinomies of existence. We are not to mistake *Molloy*'s versions of mythical and religious journeys with the truth, since they are but the narrator's little game with the traces in his mind. [51]

---

[51] In "Mercure, la mère et la mer," in *Beckett et la surdétermination littéraire* (Paris: Payot, 1977), pp. 47-70, Aldo Tagliaferri links Molloy and Lousse to a number of other mythological figures. Molloy's resemblance to Mercury is particularly stressed. In addition to the Circe, Diana, Sophia figures, Lousse is linked to Demeter Lusia. According to Tafliaferri, the Demeter and Sophia aspects of Lousse represent the positive polarities of the Mother, Circe and the Terrible Mother, the negative polarities.

Rubin Rabinovitz — "*Molloy* and the Achetypal Traveller," *Journal of Beckett Studies*, No. 5 (Autumn 1979), p. 31 — points out that the many mythical figures, to which must be added literary allusions, one superimposed on the other in the manner of a palimpsest, produce and enrich Molloy-Moran's status as an archetypal exile and traveler. Among other extensive studies of biblical and mythic figures found in *Molloy*, see Jan Hokenson, "A Stuttering Logos: Biblical Paradigms in Beckett's Trilogy," *James Joyce Quarterly*, 8 (1971), 293-310; Philip H. Solomon, *The Life after Birth: Imagery in Beckett's Trilogy* (University, Miss.: Romance Monographs, 1975); Dieter Wellershoff, "Failure of an Attempt at De-Mythologization: Samuel Beckett's Novels," trans. Martin Esslin, in *Samuel Beckett: A Collection of Critical Essays*, ed. Martin Esslin, pp. 92-107. None of the above, however, mentions Oedipus.

It is now possible to examine more closely the thematic symmetries between Molloy's and Moran's self-narrations. As already pointed out, the two share one story, the double story of the psyche, with Molloy's text chronicling what goes on within Moran. Thus, whereas Moran on the conscious level identifies with the father, views himself as a stern father, he is on the unconscious level Molloy, the son who merges with the mother. In a striking analogy to the structure of *Oedipus Rex*, Moran is like the father and simultaneously the son who killed the father and joined with his mother. And like Oedipus, Moran is both the seeker and the sought, as narrator, the teller and the told. Repeating the odyssey of many modern writers, his journey retraces the psychoanalytic path of the Oedipus tragedy.[52] In a modern parody of the kind of detective story of which the Oedipus tale is considered the prototype, Moran must search out Molloy, both absolutely other — "Tout le contraire de moi" (p. 175)/"Just the opposite of myself" (p. 113) — and an inner image of himself.[53]

Moran and Molloy thus face each other as inverted spectral doubles. Moran sees himself as a father and calls into words an inverted version of Molloy's story, foregrounding the paternal against the backdrop of Molloy's maternal space. Consequently, instead of a divine all-mother, Part II features a father-god, instead of immanence, transcendence, for the biblical exile from Eden is reenacted, actually parodied, when Gaber-Gabriel transmits Youdi-Yahweh's order for Moran first to leave his garden-paradise and then to return to it, to find Molloy and to abandon the search. Here, the paradoxical voice of the law (don't/do) belongs to an absent divine father whose voice Moran introjects: "Et la voix que j'écoute, je n'ai pas eu besoin de Gaber pour me la transmettre. Car elle est en moi..." (p. 204)./"And the voice I listen to needs no Gaber to make it heard. For it is within me..." (pp. 131-32).

---

[52] See René Girard, "De l'expérience romanesque au mythe oedipien," *Critique*, No. 222 (1965), pp. 899-924.
[53] When Robbe-Grillet based his detective novel *Les Gommes/The Erasers* (1953) on the Oedipus theme, perhaps with the ironic intention of erasing the myth, only Beckett immediately noticed the presence of the myth in the novel. See Bruce Morrissette, "Clefs pour *Les Gommes*," in *Les Gommes*, by Alain Robbe-Grillet (Paris: Union Générale d'Editions, 10/18, 1962), p. 312, n. 4.

Moran's relation to the controlling father figure is as ambiguous as Molloy's to the mother. On the one hand, Youdi is his model, since as Youdi commands him, Moran commands his son: "Tu laisseras tes deux albums à la maison.... Pas un mot de reproche, un simple futur prophétique, sur le modèle de ceux dont usait Youdi. Votre fils vous accompagnera" (p. 168)./"You leave both your albums at home.... Not a word of reproach, a simple prophetic present, on the model of those employed by Youdi. Your son goes with you" (p. 109). Moran's son in turn emulates him so that along the chain of generations sons mimic fathers: "Mon fils m'imitait instinctivement" (p. 145)./"My son imitated me instinctively" (p. 94). At the same time, the sons — Moran in his attitude toward Youdi, Jacques in his relation to Moran — hate the tyrannical fathers who exile them from their maternal enclosures (garden, house, bed) and enslave them through conflicting demands (be like me/don't be like me).

The identification with the father, with the mother, both ordered and denied by the ambiguous voices of conscience, are doubled by a visual image of the parental imprint. The hat, the stamp of the Beckettian character, on the one hand functions as the superego, literally the mark of the law of the father, and on the other, as a fragment of the womb, the caul that identifies the child with the mother. The narrator of "L'Expulsé"/"The Expelled" tells of the hat's paternal significance:

> Lorsque ma tête eut atteint ses dimensions je ne dirai pas définitives, mais maxima, mon père me dit, Viens, mon fils, nous allons acheter ton chapeau, comme s'il préexistait depuis l'éternité, dans un endroit déterminé.
>
> When my head had attained I shall not say its definitive but its maximum dimensions, my father said to me, Come, son, we are going to buy your hat, as though it had pre-existed from time immemorial in a pre-established place. [54]

The narrator emphasizes that the father picks out the hat without consulting the son, who takes this imposition as a sign that the

---

[54] *Nouvelles et "Textes pour rien,"* 2nd ed. (Paris: Minuit, 1958), p. 14./ *Stories and "Texts for Nothing"* (New York: Grove Press, 1968), p. 11.

father envies his youth. Although the hat is a mark of the father's tyranny, when the father dies the son does not throw it away: the paternal imprint is indelible.[55] On the other hand, the hat's connection to the mother comes from *Murphy*: "Murphy never wore a hat, the memories it awoke of the caul were too poignant, especially when he had to take it off" (p. 73). In accordance with the father/mother duality of Moran/Molloy, Moran appropriately fastens his hat to his head, whereas Molloy strings his to a buttonhole, suggesting an umbilical cord. The hats of Moran, connected to the father, and of Molloy, joined to the mother, repeat Watt's trying on of names, for they impose an essence, tie them to an identity (I am my father; I am my mother), rob them of their freedom.

In imitation of the father's severity, Moran, in the first part of his retrospective self-narration, depicts himself as the powerful master of his house and garden, brutalizing both his son and Marthe, his servant (whom he suspects capable of poisoning him), thus substituting a patriarchy for the matriarchal order of Lousse's domain. Moran's story is to be read by such focusing from foreground to background, the components of Molloy's story — which the reader already knows — being present but repressed in Moran's version.[56] Consequently, the events in Molloy's story serve to demystify Moran's illusions about himself. Indeed, Moran consciously believes one thing and acts out the opposite; what he says about himself is the contrary of what he does on the experiential plane, and this repressed identity — Molloy — is then projected on those around him, particularly onto Jacques: what he sees in Jacques is what he refuses to see in himself. Thus, whereas in relation to his son, Moran insists that he incarnates the law, that he is the exiler, in relation to Youdi, it is clear that

---

[55] Studies linking brain maturation with verbal and nonverbal language acquisition have shown that at roughly two years of age, after the brain has completed its major growth spurt, the child's gender has been imprinted. The passage in "L'Expulsé" could refer to this age or to puberty when brain growth levels off. See Barbara S. Wood, *Children and Comunication: Verbal and Nonverbal Language Development* (Englewood Cliffs, N. J.: Prentice-Hall, 1976), pp. 27-32.

[56] An interesting parallel is the series of figure/ground reversals depicted by Maurits C. Escher, particularly *Circle Limit IV (Heaven and Hell)*, in which interlocking bright angels and dark devils whirl into infinity.

Moran is the law's victim and the expelled, like Molloy, like Jacques. The last two mirror to Moran the unpleasant image of himself he does not want to face.

Moran's aggressivity toward his son is reenforced by a number of phallic objects, reminiscent of the sergeant's cylindrical ruler, which threaten the "I'll castrate you/you are castrated" alternatives: the lit cigar, the enema, the umbrella with which Moran beats Jacques when he refuses to abandon his bed as demanded by the father. In the latter case, Moran's anger is so intense that, having rushed outside, he hacks wildly at an old chopping-block until the axe sinks in irretrievably, a terrifying picture of the force of violence against the son, and an inverted version of Molloy's beating of the charcoal-burner. In a stroke of genius, the narration is interrupted between the beating with the umbrella and the hacking with the axe, by Moran's description of the hat on top of his head, the visible imprint of the violence of the father. Soon after this incident, Moran imagines that his son wants to kill him. And since as father and son leave the house and garden, the path is too narrow for them to walk side by side, Moran thinks of ways of tying his son to himself: "Je jouai brièvement avec l'idée de me l'attacher au moyen d'une longue corde..." (p. 199). "I toyed briefly with the idea of attaching him to me by means of a long rope..." (p. 129). [57] The verb "jouai"/"toyed" again points to the child's and Molloy's game with inverse mirror images. For, on the one hand, as the hat ties Moran to the law of the father, he in turn would tie the son to himself. The sons are, as it were, reabsorbed in the fathers. On another level, however, Moran's repressed patricidal desires and his mother identification (Molloy as his inner text) are projected onto the son, making him the opposite of the father. During the departure scene, this dual role is evident from Jacques's schoolcap which fits his head much too precisely even for Moran's taste and from the raincoat he carries rolled into a ball in front of his stomach. When one recalls Molloy's phantasy of anal birth, it comes as no surprise that Jacques's female role is emphasized during the enema scene and that Moran clearly substitutes the mother for the son in the twisted story

---

[57] In the case of the tyrant Pozzo and the slave Lucky, this idea is carried out on the stage.

(about a pilgrimage to the Madonna of Shit) he tells to the farmer on the return trek. Moran paradoxically wants to attach his son to himself and rejects him as hated rival and opposite of himself.[58]

Like the toy in the child's *fort/da* game substituted for an expelling mother, Jacques is the replacement for an expelling father in Moran's version of the game. The mirror symmetric inversion between Moran and Jacques can therefore be schematized as follows:

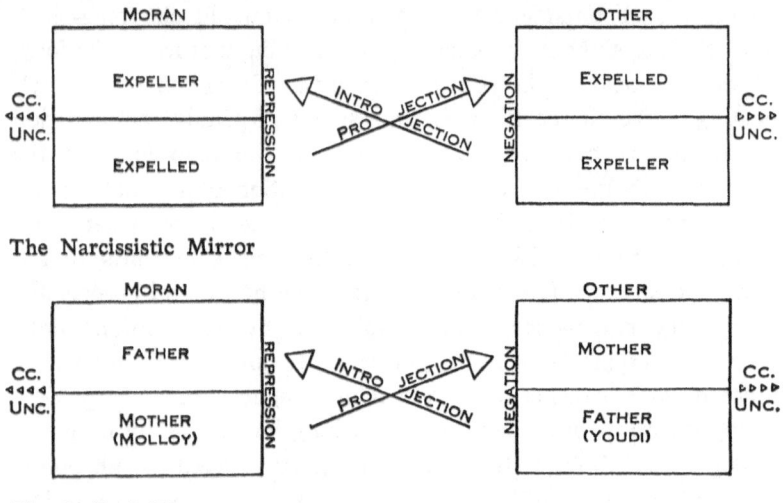

The Narcissistic Mirror

The Oedipal Mirror

Moran, refusing to recognize the unpleasant position he holds in relation to Youdi, that is, his role as victim of the law, as expelled,

---

[58] Several psychoanalytic readings of *Molloy* have emphasized Moran's homosexual stance in relation to his son. In "Toward a Psychoanalytic Reading of Beckett's *Molloy*," 2 pts., *Literature and Psychology*, 19 (1969), No. 2, 71-86; Nos. 3 and 4, 15-30, Barbara Shapiro argues that Moran desires to be a woman and struggles against unconscious homosexuality. In "On the Shores of Self: Samuel Beckett's *Molloy* — Irredentism and the Creative Impulse," *The Psychoanalytic Review*, 60 (1973), 587-604, Gilbert J. Rose draws attention to homosexual imagery in both parts of the novel, but insists on Moran's identification of his son with a woman, mentioning in particular the role of the son's raincoat as a reminder of the womb and the inverted story to the farmer. From our reading, it is clear that all the characters are bisexual and torn between the paradoxical demands, be/don't be your mother, your father.

represses it into his unconscious (the Molloy text) and projects it onto Jacques. At the same time, denying the role of expeller that Youdi takes opposite him, he introjects this pleasurable position, the inverted form of his painful role of the exiled. Consequently, like Oedipus, although he considers himself powerful and innocent, Moran is the inverse, that is Molloy, whom he fails to accept within himself, projecting instead his impotence and guilt onto his son.

Moran, for example, portrays himself as a meticulous Catholic while accusing his son of his actual impiety. By a shift of focus, however, Moran's description of receiving communion, for him a sign of his pious nature which cannot tolerate a Sunday without the sacrament, becomes an obvious example of sacrilege and a repetition of the death-of-god episode in Molloy's story. Moreover, when Moran thanks the priest for granting him a private communion, the priest replies: "Peuh... des bêtises" (p. 156)./ "Pah!...it's nothing" (p. 101). Thus, in the French version, God is reduced to a stupidity, in the English to nothing. Subsequently, several times in Moran's narration, the word "bête"/"animal" automatically brings mention of God, as for example in a particularly significant incident a few pages after the visit to the priest. While Moran (the narrator) recalls the dog Zoulou, his disgust moves from the dog to man to God: "C'est curieux, je n'aime pas les hommes et je n'aime pas les bêtes. Quant à Dieu, il commence à me dégoûter" (p. 163)./"It's a strange thing, I don't like men and I don't like animals. As for God, he is beginning to disgust me" (p. 105). Considering the multiple significance of the dog in Molloy's part and the novel's inverse mirror symmetries, it comes as no surprise that Moran (the narrated) identifies with Zoulou, phonetically a close anagram of Lousse. In case there is any doubt about the death of God, Moran later writes: "Il y a les hommes et les choses, ne me parlez pas des animaux. Ni de Dieu" (p. 256)./"There are men and there are things, to hell with animals. And with God" (p. 165).

And again, although Moran suspects his son of wanting to kill him, in a repetition of Molloy's Oedipal murders, Moran hallucinates killing the part of himself that most closely mirrors his conscious identity of father. During the three days his son is away at Hole to buy a bicycle, Moran, as we have seen, comes face to face with two parts of himself, thus giving his version of the A and B encounter at the beginnig of Molloy's narrative (complete to the details of A's dog and B's club). When the dim man, the one who is hunting down the old man with the stick, as Moran hunts Molloy, encouraged by Moran's limp, bars his way to what Moran terms his "petite maison"/"little house" (p. 230/p. 148) and threatens him with his hand, Moran kills him in a frenzy. The components of the Oedipus story — the aggressive man, whom the limping Moran resembles, blocking the path to the maternal house — are carefully built into the episode whose hallucinatory quality is underscored by the haziness of the sounds and figures Moran perceives. Here again, an event inscribed in Molloy's narration, that is, the beating of the charcoal burner, figures the repressed script that Moran reads when in a dream-like or trance-like state. It is an event which he consciously acts out in inverse (the beating of his son and the chopping-block) and which he projects onto others (it is his son who wants to kill him).

In this episode, as throughout the two part novel, the inverted mirror images of the *fort/da* game, pitting the mythic father-son and mother-son polarities against each other, are linked to a number of cosmic dualities, sky and earth, sun and moon, day and night, order and disorder, and particularly fire and water. Throughout, the father figures are related to fire: Molloy calls the man in the forest a charcoal-burner because he sees smoke, and both A and Moran carry lit cigars. The dim man, who is later killed, accosts Moran just as he has lit his fire, whereas the man with the club approached in darkness. Generally, Moran's days around the campfire parallel Molloy's time at the sea. One could compare, as well, Moran's reflection on sixteen startling theological questions (related to the transcendent father) with Molloy's seaside diversion with sixteen sucking stones (a mother-related activity). And whereas Moran sees himself a fiery torch next to the campfire (p. 228/p. 147), Molloy imagines putting out to sea never to return (p. 104/p. 69). (The narrator of *From an Abandoned Work* — written in the early fifties — is similarly haunted by the possibilities, on the one hand, of the two mother-and father-related deaths — "And that is perhaps how I shall die at last if they don't catch me, I mean drowned, or in fire..." — and on the other, by the contrary, by the double violence against the father and the mother:

"My father, did I kill him too as well as my mother, perhaps in a way I did...."). [59] In *Molloy*, the cosmic dualities underline the repetitions and oppositions of the two narratives.

After hallucinating the death of the father and following his loss of faith, Moran experiences great inner metamorphoses which, since they repeat Molloy's tumbles during his violent encounters with Lousse's dog and the charcoal-burner, are likened to a fall (p. 241/p. 155). As a consequence of his mythic three-day descent into the inner depths (Moran's version of the *descente en enfer*), the paternal image dissolves and Moran begins to resemble Molloy. During Moran's return journey, then, as in Molloy's, darkness, water, physical decay, disorder, and confusion predominate. (His circular journey from garden to garden covers the regression/progression to womb and tomb.) And like Molloy, Moran meets with father-like obstacles, "les hommes méchants et les spectres qui voulurent m'empêcher de rentrer chez moi, comme Youdi me l'avait enjoint" (p. 258)/"the fiends in human shape and the phantoms of the dead that tried to prevent me from getting home, in obedience to Youdi's command" (p. 166). Thus, the confrontation with the farmer, in bowler hat, who stops Moran shortly before he reaches his garden and who is most likely the same man who had earlier insisted on driving Moran and his son back home, bristles with references to Molloy's encounters and to the paradoxical situation of the Oedipus story.

---

[59] *First Love and Other Shorts* (New York: Grove Press, 1974), pp. 40 and 44. Using the same imagery, Krapp — *Krapp's Last Tape and Other Dramatic Pieces* (New York: Grove Press, 1958), p. 25 — speaks of himself as "drowned in dreams and burning to be gone."

For further discussion of light/dark imagery in Beckett's works, see James Knowlson, *Light and Darkness in the Theatre of Samuel Beckett* (London: Turret Books, 1972); and Edouard Morot-Sir, "Samuel Beckett and Cartesian Emblems," in *Samuel Beckett: The Art of Rhetoric*, pp. 25-104. In the latter article, especially on pp. 78-92, Morot-Sir convincingly links Beckett's play with light and darkness to Manichaeism or the Gnosis. Of the Beckettian characters, Morot-Sir (p. 84) holds: "Their secret is the meaning of Beckett's asceticism, which originates, not in the Stoics and their distinction between things which depend upon us and those that don't, and not in the Christian ideal of pure love *(agapé)* but in the Manichaean sense of obligation to separate the light and the dark as the primordial dualities of being and nothingness." That instead of separation or union the characters attain a "mingling" of light and dark, as pointed out by Morot-Sir, is also true of Moran-Molloy.

And yet, Moran continues nevertheless to be the opposite of Molloy: he bullies his son, is mistaken for the butcher among the lambs — Molloy is taken for a sacrificial victim — is recognized as Moran. From our reading, it is clear that Moran does not *become* Molloy, since Molloy is at all times a repressed part of Moran.[60] During his travels Moran has come to the borderline of Molloy's territory, the zone between consciousness and the unconscious, has recognized the movements, the strange forces within this region, without, however, reaching them, since as he writes, he never saw that "Obidil" (an anagram of libido) either "de près"/"face to face," as he had hoped, or "de loin"/"darkly" (p. 251/p. 162). Thus, the inner forces, the Obidil/libido, which Moran had envisioned as working on him from without in the form of the tyrannical Youdi, escape him, remain unknown to him, as did Knott for Watt. The allusion to I Corinthians 13.12 ("For now we see through a glass, darkly; but then face to face: now I know in part; but then shall I know even as also I am known"), particularly in the English version, links Moran's search, like Watt's for Knott, to a quest beyond a mirror image of self. Like all the other Beckettian versions of this quest, however, Moran/Molloy's does not reach an end, but regresses to a point where it is yet to begin.

It is clear by this time that Moran's search for Molloy, Molloy's for his mother, are one and the same quest pursued on different psychic levels. Molloy's identification with the mother and the

---

[60] In "Moran-Molloy: The Hero as Author," *Perspective,* 11 (Autumn 1959), 183-93, Edith Kern, in an argument taken up by many critics, holds that, chronologically, the first part of *Molloy* follows the second part, and that Moran turns into Molloy. Although early in the article, Kern (p. 186) points out that "Molloy's 'visitations' represent, undoubtedly, the stirrings within Moran of a subconscious, antithetical self," and ties Moran's journey to the myth of the "one hero in two aspects," she nevertheless argues (p. 189) that "the author-hero Molloy continues the journey begun by the author-hero Moran." According to my reading, to the contrary, the two parts are a psychic double text, the unconscious repressed version preceding the conscious rendition in order to make a double reading possible and also in order to suggest that the primary process precedes the secondary process in the manner the child is father to the man. Indeed, Moran speaks of his hope that "Molloy... viendrait jusqu'à moi, qui n'avais su aller jusqu'à lui, et que j'en ferais un ami, un père..." (p. 251)./ "Molloy... would come to me, who had not been able to get to him, and to grow to be a friend, and like a father to me..." (pp. 161-62).

similarity between the uncertain names of Molloy-Mollose and Loy-Lousse all point to this oneness which, moreover, Moran perceives:

> La mère Molloy, ou Mollose, ne m'était pas non plus complètement étrangère, il me semblait.... Après tout je ne savais peut-être rien de la mère Molloy, ou Mollose, sauf dans la mesure où un tel fils en porte les traces, comme des lambeaux de coiffe. (p. 173)
>
> Mother Molloy, or Mollose, was not completely foreign to me either, it seemed.... After all perhaps I knew nothing of mother Molloy, or Mollose, save in so far as such a son might bear, like a scurf of placenta, her stamp. (p. 112) [61]

Consequently, Moran's descent into his unconscious in search of Molloy, a descent carefully staged as a somnolent state between waking and dreaming, and likened to an inner journey through a garden landscape, vertically mirrors Molloy's crossing the threshold into the psyche. (One might even mention the humorous detail of the cows that Molloy imagines at the beginning of his inner journey reappearing as oxen [castrated bulls] in Moran's rendition [p. 172/p. 111]). Moran/Molly's quest is, moreover, only the latest in a series, since Molloy is only one of a number of inner images

---

[61] It has been shown that from a mythical and biological perspective, it is the placenta which, being common to mother and child, brings them into the relationship of identity. In *Capitalisme et schizophrénie: L'Anti-Oedipe* (Paris: Minuit, 1972), p. 186, Gilles Deleuze and Félix Guattari write: "C'est que le placenta, en tant que substance commune à la mère et à l'enfant, partie commune de leur corps, fait que ces corps ne sont pas comme une cause et un effet, mais tous deux produits dérivés de cette même substance par rapport à laquelle le fils est jumeau de sa mère.... Oui, j'ai été ma mère et j'ai été mon fils." The translation by Robert Hurley, Mark Seem, and Helen R. Lane — *Capitalism and Schizophrenia: Anti-Oedipus* (New York: Viking, 1977), p. 158 — reads as follows: "It is because the placenta, as a substance common to the mother and the child, a common part of their bodies, makes it such that these bodies are not like cause and effect, but are both products derived from this same substance, in relation to which the son is his mother's twin.... Yes, I have been my mother and I have been my son." Moreover, according to Deleuze and Guattari, this impersonal, germinal substance is desired beyond the mother, a fundamental desire repressed in the classical Freudian interpretation of the Oedipus myth. Deleuze and Guattari quote from Beckett's novels throughout the book and obviously admire his playful manipulation of schizophrenic and oedipal materials.

tracked down by Moran, the latest of a whole "galerie de crevés"/ "gallery of moribunds" like Murphy, Watt, Yerk, and Mercier (p. 212/p. 137). And just as in the case of *Watt,* Moran's search for Molloy and Molloy's for his mother are but the moments of an infinite chain of regression to the unknowable. Thus, Moran is and is not Molloy who is and is not his mother who is and is not the end of the quest, for finally, the quest aims beyond all personal identifications to anonymous traces within. Moran had therefore been uncertain at first what to call the inner movements he perceives, the incessant, chaotic activity to which no name, age, sex, or personal identity could be applied. The name Molloy, imposed by Youdi/Gaber, and the mother-quest, ordered by inner imperatives, were but faulty translations of the still unnamable.

As a consequence, the paradoxical bind of the oedipal imperatives, precipitating the narcissistic play with mirror inversions of self, is rejected by both narrators. And it is outside the mythic mother and father poles of immanence and transcendence that they might be able to free themselves from their bond to violence, from the projection of the repressed and the introjection of cruelty. Thus, at the end of his self-narration, Moran no longer identifies the voice he hears with a transcendent father nor with the inner bureaucracy of the superego, for he says of the voice: "Elle ne se servait pas des mots qu'on avait appris au petit Moran, que lui à son tour avait appris à son petit" (p. 272)./"It did not use the words that Moran had been taught when he was little and that he in his turn had taught to his little one" (p. 176). This impersonal voice, like Molloy's "quelque chose de changé dans le silence" (p. 135/"something gone wrong with the silence" (p. 88), functions outside the mother-father-child matrix, so that one can link it to a call for exteriority rejecting the enclosing spaces of the past for the infinite play of differences between male and female, light and dark, order and disorder, life and death, preferring not one duality *or* the other, nor one *and* the other reunited or synthesized into a totality, but the play of infinite possibilities.[62] It is this anon-

---

[62] The concept of exteriority comes from Emmanuel Lévinas, *Totalité et infini: Essai sur l'extériorité,* 4th ed. (The Hague: Martinus Nijhoff, 1974).

ymous voice which he is just beginning to understand that makes Moran wonder at the end whether he is perhaps more free.

Since it is also this voice which commanded Moran to write his report, an attempt is made to remove writing from the control of the paternal logos. That writing is linked on the one hand to phallic aggression and on the other to rematriation is clear from *Molloy*'s narrator writing in his mother's room (in an unborn state) under the orders of the master. The situation of the preamble's narrator (chronologically the last moment of the novel) is that of a writer about to die, about to be born from his own womb. *Molloy* can indeed be read as writing about the genesis of the artistic and particularly the writing process. In the *Hidden Order of Art,* Anton Ehrenzweig theorizes that the projection/introjection alternation, whose function Melanie Klein described (and which Gear and Liendo linked to the *fort/da* game), is at work both in interpersonal relations and in the relationship of artists to their works. In the chapter entitled "The Three Phases of Creativity," Ehrenzweig describes a first phase in which artists project fragmented or split-off parts of their persons into the work. Since artists perceive these fragments as foreign and persecuting, this stage is termed "paranoid-schizoid." The second phase, called "manic," under the control of the primary process, strives to heal the fragmentation through undifferentiation and gives rise to what Freud termed the "oceanic" feeling of union with the universe. At this stage, "the work acts as a receiving 'womb' " which then "integrates the fragments into a coherent whole (the unconscious substructure or matrix of the work of art)." In the third or "depressive" phase, the artist re-introjects the hidden matrix at a near-conscious level. Ehrenzweig concludes:

> In this manner a full exchange occurs between the conscious and unconscious components of the work as well as between the artist's conscious and unconscious levels of perception. His own unconscious also serves as a 'womb' to receive split-off and repressed parts of his conscious self. The external [in the work] and the internal [in the artist's psyche] processes of integration are dif-

ferent aspects of the same indivisible process of creativity.[63]

In *Molloy,* Moran's part corresponds quite strikingly to Ehrenzweig's first stage, to the projection of fragmented parts of himself into his narrative, that is, of the paternal logos with which he identifies (Youdi) and the maternal imperative which he represses (Molloy), both of which moreover, he perceives as hostile. When Moran (the conscious part of the narrator) permits himself contact with Molloy (the unconscious) there is a movement toward the undifferentiation of the second phase, an undifferentiation Molloy achieves in his enwombing. The narrator of the preamble then would seem to attempt the third phase, the reintrojection of Molloy (the repressed material) on a conscious level through giving birth to himself from the womb of his writing. (The parallel, apparent since *Watt,* between writing and the work of psychic forces, between the external and inner processes, will become the central theme of *Malone meurt.*)

In Beckett's works, however, as we have seen, the synthesizing solutions whether they be those of philosophy, religion, myth, psychology, or art no longer apply. No new order emerges from a reconciliation of opposing forces or the descent into the inner depth, the poetic *descente en enfer.* For it is beyond the clash of the old dualities not from them that the Beckettian narrator seeks to be born. It is this utopic process that the writing pursues, in the meanwhile turning the old themes into the playthings of the narrator's pen. The come and go continue.

Thus, Malone writing in Molloy's room likens it to a head and a womb, that is, the work's matrix from which he will either die, be born, or both. Contained within this scriptural space, Malone in turn contains a text he is writing: he is giving birth/death at the same time as he is being born/dying. Throughout the novel, the pendular swings move between the poles of life and death, throughout it is uncertain whether Malone awaits death or birth. The first sentence of the novel announces Malone's imminent death ("Je serai quand même bientôt tout à fait mort enfin."/"I shall soon be quite dead at last in spite of all.") and the final words

---

[63] The quotes in the above paragraph are taken from *The Hidden Order of Art* (Berkeley: Univ. of California Press, 1968), pp. 104-05.

"plus rien"/"never anything/there/any more" point to its accomplishment. Yet at other times, Malone imagines himself heading for birth, since he sees the ceiling rhythmically moving in and out, hears the rush of water, and concludes: "Je nais dans la mort.... Drôle de gestation" (p. 208)./"I am given... birth to into death" (p. 283). (Beckett omitted the "strange pregnancy" of the French version.) As usual, then, the antithetical positions dissolve: Malone pictures himself as an old fetus within a dead womb about to be born into the charnel-house (p. 94/p. 225) (a variant on the image of birth astride a grave found in *Godot*) or imagines his stillbirth, being carried head-first out of the room (pp. 114-15/p. 235). Malone thus paradoxically must either die in order to be born or be born in order to die, a paradox that all the former games and pastimes have played through and on which Malone will concentrate.

The come and go between Eros and Thanatos is familiar from *Molloy* and the earlier *Nouvelles*. In "L'Expulsé," the narrator, like Malone, would condense birth and death into one moment: "Je serais volontiers mort dans cette maison. Je vis, dans une sorte de vision, la porte s'ouvrir et mes pieds sortir" (p. 17)./"I would have gladly died in that house. In a sort of vision I saw the door open and my feet come out" (p. 12). On the other hand, the narrator of "La Fin"/"The End," snugly enclosed in his boat, envisions the water rising slowly to cover him, "drowned in dreams" like Krapp, the dream of the return to the womb. Is Malone at the end born into death or does he die to be born? As in the other novels, no resolution of the conflict comes about; the end, Malone's death/birth, is but one moment in the continous game of come and go: yes, I am about to die; no, I am about to be born. The birthing/dying of the narrator from the womb of writing is endlessly postponed.

Malone's three ways of playing with self-presence, descriptions of his present state (self-proximity), writing stories (self-identity), and the inventory of his possesions (self-possession), all link writing with the life and death paradox. Accordingly, the three versions of *fort/da* play accumulate cosmic, religious, and literary references to birth, death, and rebirth. At the beginning of his self-narration, Malone thinks he will die in the Spring — April or May — if not at some equally symbolic moment in the Summer, mentioning Saint John the Baptist's day, the Fourteenth of July, the Transfiguration, and the Assumption as possibilities. Later, on hearing a mixed choir, Malone, echoing Faust, supposes it is Easter week and that the song honors "celui qui le premier ressuscita d'entre les morts" (p. 62)/"him who was the first to rise from the dead" (p. 208), implying that his death too will lead to resurrection.

On the level of the stories Malone tells, the Louis/Lambert family, cultivating the life-giving earth ("la terre nourricière" is specified by the French version on page 57), through the monotonous round of seasons, introduces the cosmic theme of the continuous rebirth of seeds in the earth. Moreover, for this farm family the Christmas season stands out as the commemoration of the Savior's birth, but for the father, another in the series of butchers, it promises the long anticipated moment when he will be able to kill pigs. "Il était réputé bon saigneur..." (p. 46)/"He was highly thought of as a bleeder..." (p. 199), the text puts it, which is a ferocious pun — *seigneur*/lord, *saigneur*/bleeder — in the French. The juxtaposition of these two events, Christ's birth and animal slaughter (a popular French brand of pork sausage is named "B. B. Jésus de Lyon") recalls Beckett's repeated emphasis on Christ as a sacrificial scapegoat.[64] For the same reason, Malone's persona Macmann, "the son of man," is first named Saposcat, an anagram of "scapegoat." Thus, the farm family's butchery of animals (goats among them) counteracts their life-producing cultivation of the earth. Only in the case of the mule, saved by Louis/Lambert from the slaughter-house, are death and rebirth reconciled. For while burying the mule, he thinks of the tendency of the buried and the drowned to rise again to the surface.

Then, in the second part of the story, when Macmann is surprised by a violent rain in a barren landscape, he first faces and clutches the earth, with arms outstretched, then turns over and accepts the beating from the sky. In a reversal of the ordinary guilt-punishment sequence, the physical action of the rain and the sacrificial posture of his body evoke in Macmann first the

---

[64] The label of the *Melli B. B. Jésus de Lyon* explains that the name goes back to the time of Henri IV when Lyon was famous for its pork sausage. Since the sausage was prepared and eaten at Christmas time and bundled like the Infant Christ, it was given his name. In this connection, one might add that Beckett's Louis/Lambert is the opposite of Balzac's character in the novel by that name. The Christmas butcher mocks Louis Lambert's dictum that flesh will be made word.

idea of punishment, as if water, the element of purification, necessarily implied guilt. As wavering as Malone about life and death, Macmann cannot determine whether life is the sin or the punishment for sin, or again if birth is the original sin or the original expiation, or indeed if they are not part of an unending series of sinful atonements. For Macmann, consequently, the baptismal rains represent simultaneously the fault itself and the punishment that promises salvation, strikingly evoked in this passage by the fiery element, the stars which would eventually light his way. Earth, sky, water, and fire alternate powerfully in this condensed drama of suffering, of sin and redemption, life and death.

This episode echoes one of Malone's most harmonious memories:

> Et cependant il me semble que je suis né et que j'ai vécu longuement... et que j'ai été longuement au bord des mers en pleurs devant les îles et péninsules où venaient briller la nuit les petites lumières jaunes et brèves des hommes... (p. 95).

> And yet it sometimes seems to me I did get born and had a long life... and tarried by the seas in tears before the islands and peninsulas where night lit the little brief yellow lights of man... (pp. 225-6).

And finally the same landscape, which reappears in many of Beckett's fictions — sea, islands, stars and lights on the mountains — with its contrasting dark and light, water and fire, deep and high, sea and land, announces the final scene of both the story and novel in which a series of inmates of the writer's asylum-psyche are taken on an Easter excursion. (The time and place evoke Beckett's birth during Easter week and Dante's Easter ascent in the *Divine Comedy*.) At nightfall, after the six characters have entered the sea, as the water and darkness engulf them, the lights flicker in the sky, on the land. Huddled together, an undifferentiated mass, these fragments of the writer's psyche sink into the dark and silent womb in which they remain still unborn. The narrator, through his stories, instead of achieving re-integration or rebirth leaves off with the "gone" position of the game until the next move.

Throughout the novel, then, on the different narrative levels, the fertile earth, the life-giving water, the pregnant dark, the promise of light, the cycle of seasons, as well as the two celebrations of birth and rebirth, Christmas and Easter, are set against the devouring earth, sea, and dark, the invading light, and sacrificial death. The to and fro between the paradoxical light and dark still seems the favorite game. Within Malone's self-narration, he is uncertain whether it is day or night in his room, since he lies in the inner gloom where consciousness and the unconscious meet. And in Malone's self-reflexive fiictions, Sapo watches a gray or "ashen" hen move back and forth across the threshold dividing the dark kitchen from the light ouside, and on his wanderings, Sapo in turn, is shown "passant de l'ombre à la clarté, de la clarté à l'ombre, avec indifférence" (p. 58)./"passing from light to shadow, from shadow to light, unheedingly" (p. 206).

When Malone enumerates his possessions, it becomes even more apparent how closely interrelated the three games are with the writing process and the writing in turn with the life/death antinomies. A stick, given to Malone by the old woman who fed and took care of him, the mother-figure who appears and disappears from his room, permits him to make his possessions, the fragments of his past, these broken toys — the bowl of a pipe missing a stem, one faded boot, a brimless hat, the cap of a bicycle bell, the top half of one crutch, and so on — come and go in the manner of the abandoned child's game. The possessions, like the unknowable forces within, are in constant flux: some disappear, some appear of which he has no memory, and others (like universal archetypes) may be present without his knowledge. As a consequence, since he is forever uncertain of what he possesses, he cannot piece together an accurate description, a total text. And when Malone finally loses the stick (reminiscent of lost ladders and bicycles) the link to his possessions is broken, the game suspended.

Foremost among his possessions, however, Malone draws attention to the little Venus pencil with which he is writing the novel's text into a child's exercise book. Immediately after he first mentions the pencil and notebook in his self-narration, Malone describes in detail the "Blackbird"/"Bird" fountain-pen Mr. Saposcat is to give his son for his examinations. The sexual symbolic meaning of writing materials has been pointed out by Melanie Klein:

> The maternal significance of dais and also of desk and slate and everything that can be written upon, as well as the penis-meaning of penholder, slate-pencil and chalk, and of everything with which one can write, became so evident for me... and was so constantly confirmed that I consider it to be *typical*.[65]

In *Malone meurt,* the names of both pencil and pen underline the sexual significance of the objects. On both narrative levels, then, it is clear that writing is derived from an unconscious incest wish which has been sublimated. Certainly, Malone's writing in his notebook, within the mother's bed, enclosed in a womblike space, evokes the incestual relation. And within Malone's fictions, since writing is too closely linked to what he dreads, Sapo prefers watching the soaring of hawks in the sky to doing his schoolwork. Later, however, Macmann's grotesque copulation with Mag-like Moll — "d'une parfaite impuissance l'un et l'autre" (p. 163)/"both were completely impotent" (p. 260) — mirrors and mocks Malone's project of writing himself into life through the insemination of the exercise book he calls his life. For instead of an insemination, writing is a dissemination, is linked not to impregnation but to impotence, and, as we have seen, to playing with the self.[66]

On the other hand, Malone's pencil is linked to a number of weapons of death. (Melanie Klein speculated that "at the root of the sexual-symbolic meaning of the penholder lay probably originally that of the weapon and the hand.")[67] From this point of view, writing is the sublimation of aggressive drives, linked to Thanatos, and helps to explain the frequently repeated Beckettian motif that writing is a punishment imposed by one or a series of cruel masters. The blows the narrators inflict on themselves and the reciprocal violence among fragmented parts serve to underscore this theme. Indeed, Malone writes of an apparition that

---

[65] "The Rôle of the School in the Libidinal Development of the Child" (1923), in *Love, Guilt and Reparation,* p. 60, n. 1. In the postscript to "La Scène de l'écriture," in *L'Écriture et la différence,* p. 340, Jacques Derrida writes that the above article by Klein possibly points the way toward a new "graphologie psychanalytique."

[66] For an analysis of writing as dissemination, see Jacques Derrida, "La Double Séance," in *La Dissémination* (Paris: Seuil, 1972), pp. 199-318.

[67] "The Rôle of the School in the Libidinal Development of the Child," pp. 66-67.

hits him on the head and then in turn of Lemuel's blows against himself and the asylum inmates. And after having wondered at one point how many of his personae (the line going back to Murphy at least) he has killed, Malone proceeds to write the scene in which the reassembled psychic inmates die with him at the end. At this point, the pencil writing the death scene of the sailors Lemuel kills and of the characters in the boat is compared with the murderous hatchet, hammer, stick, and fist.

It is interesting to note that Melanie Klein has chronicled a number of phantasies connected to writing that intriguingly resemble the Beckettian motifs of pencil and exercise book, of boats and the sea, and of bicycles and routes. About her patient Fritz (about six years old at the time), she writes:

> [I]n his phantasies the lines in his exercise book were roads, the book itself was the whole world and the letters rode into it on motor bicycles, *i.e.*, on the pen. Again, the pen was a boat and the exercise book a lake.... We discovered that the spoken word was to him identical with the written. The word stood for the penis or the child, while the movement of the tongue and the pen stood for coitus.[68]

So that *Molloy*'s bicycle(s), *Malone meurt*'s boat and stick (connecting him to his possessions) can be read along with the clubs, umbrellas, fists, hammers, and crutches as symbolic writing vehicles, the former emphasizing writing as a route into the psyche-womb, the latter as the blow of death, a conflict never resolved in favor of one or the other conception. (Malone's Venus is, of course, an instrument of both life and death.)

On the one hand, then, under the control of the maternal imperative, writing opens a path into the psyche in search of a text inscribed in the past and whose significance the present text must reconstitute. The unconscious writing within, however, is only one of an infinite series of partial texts so that meaning — as shown by Derrida — is ever deferred and replaced by play. The writing process, however, is also ordered by the paradoxical voices, linked both to the incest wish (going to the mother) and to the forceful imposition of the paternal logos ("be like the father").

---

[68] "Early Analysis" (1923), in *Love, Guilt and Reparation*, p. 100.

Since, as we have seen, these imperatives are contradicted by the maternal and paternal commands ("don't be like the father"), writing is a form of the double bind, an activity both desired and imposed, both good and bad, promising on the one hand rebirth, reparation and atonement, and on the other guilt and death. The writer, a modern Oedipus struggling with these conflicting desires and demands, seeking a way out of this maddening impasse, resorts in the meanwhile to the double alibi of the game, a temporary respite from the prison of voices.

In *L'Innommable,* it is indeed the words themselves which the narrator indicts. It is they which — more accurately than the ladder, vehicle, and tool metaphors of old — make the writer's task impossible. Impossible in two ways: first, there are no words to name the unnamable, to reconstitute the unconscious script into other than a travesty of itself, a theme familiar since *Watt.* Language is finally only a ladder of smoke, "des mots comme faits de fumée" (p. 131) / "words like smoke" (p. 77), according to the voice of *Textes pour rien.*

And secondly, the words at his disposal are those of hostile forces speaking through him, "des ennemis qui m'habitent" (p. 123) / "the voices and thoughts of the devils who beset me" (p. 347), turning him into one of the incompetent parrots that chatter throughout the novels. And although the words are imposed on him, and like the hats, imprint someone else's text, tie him to the others, make him like others, they do not "fit": "quelqu'un dit on, c'est la faute des pronoms, il n'y a pas de nom pour moi, pas de pronom pour moi..." (p. 240). / "someone says you, it's the fault of the pronouns, there is no name for me, no pronoun for me..." (p. 404). As a consequence, the narrator, trapped in the web of words that cannot speak him except as what he is not, repeats versions of the former games at a frantic pace, while concentrating on the come and go between words and silence.

Inventing two opposing personae, the Unnamable strongly denies that he may be identified with one or the other. He cannot wear the new names Basile (king), soon changed to Mahood (mankind), and the "anti-Mahood" Worm: "L'essentiel est que je n'arrive jamais nulle part, que je ne sois jamais nulle part, ni chez Mahood, ni chez Worm, ni chez moi..." (p. 105). / "The essential is never to arrive anywhere, never to be anywhere, neither where Mahood is, nor where Worm is, nor where I am..." (p. 338). He is not to be confused with mankind, with Mahood and his cruel stories, nor with Worm's silence of non-existence. The Unnamable only plays at being one and the other — like Mahood he is made of words, "je suis fait de mots, des mots des autres" (p. 204) / "I'm... made of words, others' words" (p. 386); and he is silent, "Non, je n'ai pas de voix.... C'est une des raisons pour lesquelles je me suis confondu avec Worm" (p. 123) / "No, I have no voice.... That's one of the reasons why I confused myself with Worm" (p. 347) — before he rejects both.

There are a few allusions as well to the old Logos (in the Knott and Youdi tradition), the master, "à mon image" (p. 51) / "in my image" (p. 312), the narrator teases, who imposes writing as a pensum, who knows the redeeming words for which the Unnamable listens in vain: "j'ai parlé pour mon maître, j'ai dressé l'oreille pour les paroles de mon maître, jamais venues" (p. 47). / "I have spoken for my master, listened for the words of my master never spoken" (p. 310). On the opposite pole from the master's total text and Mahood's stream of words, the Unnamable explores Worm's womb of silence:

> Vite un endroit. Sans accès, sans issue, endroit sûr. Pas comme l'Eden. Et Worm dedans. Ne sentant rien, ne sachant rien, ne pouvant rien, ne voulant rien. Jusqu'au moment où il entend ce bruit qui ne cessera plus. Alors c'est la fin, Worm n'est plus. (p. 126)

> Quick, a place. With no way in, no way out, a safe place. Not like Eden. And Worm inside. Feeling nothing, knowing nothing, capable of nothing, wanting nothing. Until the instant he hears the sound that will never stop. Then it's the end, Worm no longer is. (pp. 348-49)

Thus, the silent Worm is eternally in an unborn, never-to-be-born, state. And although it was easy to speak of Mahood on his travels and in his jar and invent this human fiction in words, it is impossible to speak of the non-existing Worm. How is one to speak of the silence of nothingness? As soon as the Unnamable speaks of Worm, he speaks of him as if he were Mahood, somebody instead of nobody. There is no way. Finally, neither the Master-Word, nor the Nirvana-Silence, nor the human voices speaking through him free the Unnamable from his prison of paradox.

The Unnamable, moreover, is not only nameless, but also bodyless. He is the latest stage in the characters' long dehumanization: Murphy did not look human to his prospective employers; Watt, at first sight undistinguishable from a parcel or a carpet, could no longer call himself a man; Moran-Molloy-Malone evolve from two-legged, to three-legged, to four-legged creatures to an undifferentiated fetal state. The unhuman Unnamable, then, oscillating between Mahood (a fragmented body) and Worm (no-body) makes various organs come and go. At first, he imagines himself with his hands on his knees, looking straight ahead, then, after all the other organs have fallen off, he concentrates on his tear-streaming eyes which are replaced by a mouth, until it disappears in turn. The eyes vie in importance with the mouth, since the eyes weep as the mouth speaks its suffering: "C'est un flot ininterrompu, de mots et de larmes.... mes mots sont mes larmes, mes yeux ma bouche," says the narrator of *Textes pour rien* (p. 181) / "It's an unbroken flow of words and tears.... my words are my tears, my eyes my mouth" (p. 111). This confusion of eyes and mouth recall the other between vagina and anus in *Molloy*, between being born and being shat, a link accomplished in the *Textes* as well where the mouth is identified with the anus, words with excrement (p. 197 / p. 123). Writing, then, and the Unnamable insists that he is writing, is like being born, shat, spoken, or wept.

On the other hand, the look of others like the words of others seek to pin the Unnamable to a human identity: "Sans ouvrir la bouche, rien qu'en me fixant avec ses yeux... il [Basile] me rendait chaque fois un peu plus tel qu'il me voulait" (p. 22). / "Without opening his mouth, fastening on me his eyes... he [Basil] changed me a little more each time into what he wanted me to be" (p. 298).[69] Subsequently, in the Mahood stories, it is the eyes of the mother-figure, Marguerite-Madeleine, that keep this human caricature in a jar in existence. When she no longer comes to look at him, he disappears. The Unnamable rejects the eyes as such, whether the image of life (the tear-filled sockets), the aggressively evil eye, or the source of life, for although he concedes that to

---

[69] Whereas the Sartrean look dehumanizes, metamorphosizing the victim into a beast or a thing, the Beckettian look, paradoxically, anthropomorphizes.

be human is to be perceived, to be born is to be born into language and tears, where the Unnamable is (yet-to-be-born unlike the badly born Mahood and the never-to-be-born Worm) cannot be reached through language or perception. Were the Unnamable in search of human identity, it? she? he? (obviously no pronoun works for this impersonal force) would accept the words spoken through it, the old images and myths, the old desire, violence, and delusions projected into it. Instead, the Beckettian text aims to give birth to what is yet unknown, yet to begin, a project that *Comment c'est* recommences.

The narrator of this last full-length novel resembles an abandoned senescent infant who plays through once again the old game with new models of the same toys. The inner playground of darkness and primeval mud recalls what Joseph Campbell describes as "the second womb, the matrix of the postnatal gestation of the placental *Homo sapiens*."[70] Indeed, the novel's unnamed narrator would seem to head toward birth like Malone: he imagines crawling from west to east, "c'est curieux alors qu'à l'ouest la mort en général" (p. 149) / "strange and death in the west as a rule" (p. 123). Halfway through the text, he postulates just such a birth for himself from the mud:

> l'impression d'être né plutôt octogénaire à l'âge où l'on meurt dans le noir la boue en remontant né en remontant en faisant surface comme les noyés (p. 87)
>
> the feeling rather of having been born octogenarian at the age when one dies in the dark the mud upwards born upwards floating up like the drowned (p. 70)

But no, the unnamed narrator, like all the others is not yet born at the end and remains stuck in a prison-womb of words, of paradoxical voices (one refrain repeats, "j'entends dire que oui puis que non" / "I hear yes then no"), darkness, and a false present which has been compared to Hegel's "bad infinity" *(schlechte Unendlichkeit).*[71] So he plays with light and dark, recalling glim-

---

[70] "Bios and Mythos," p. 21.
[71] See Hans-Joachim Schulz, *This Hell of Stories: A Hegelian Approach to the Novels of Samuel Beckett* (The Hague: Mouton, 1973), pp. 106-11. Schulz points out that Dieter Wellershoff — *Der Gleichgültige: Versuche*

merings from the past, both memories and fictions, and then extinguishes them; time and timelessness, writing in past and future tenses which the present swallows up; and has another caper with Eros, Thanatos, and Logos.

The love object is specifically the sack (already familiar from *Mercier et Camier*) that nourishes, comforts, and envelops him. He would like to enter it so that his head touches the end like a caul; he hangs it from his neck with a cord (like formerly the hat) and then like the abandoned child's toy makes it disappear at the end.

The hostility (interspersed with moments of tenderness) is staged by means of generations of tormentors and victims, tormentors who become victims, victims who become tormentors, the old chain of violent relationships. The narrator, in the second part, depicts one such encounter, with himself in the role of the aggressor. The interaction between the antagonists intensifies the cruelty of father/son, writer/persona relationships found in the previous novels and identifies socio-symbolic inscription with stimulus-response training and aggression. The education of the victim can be divided into four stages:

1. *The pre-linguistic stage*

The tormentor digs his nails into the victim's armpit to force him to abandon cries for song. This stage corresponds to the time at around eight months when infants begin to echo their parents' intonation patterns, the musical aspect of language.

über Hemingway, Camus, Benn und Beckett (Köln: Kiepenheuer und Witsch, 1963), p. 121 — first mentioned Hegel's bad infinity in relation to Beckett. On the link between infinity and the motif of the journey without a goal, Manfred Frank — "The Infinite Text," trans. Michael Schwerin, *Glyph*, 7 (1980), p. 96 — writes: "The self-disintegration of textual economy... becomes the *'epideixis* of infinity.' An infinity, it is true, which, after the loss of a transcendental economy of salvation and return *(Heimkehr)*, can manifest itself only in the form of Hegel's *bad infinity:* as the thorn of yearning woven or driven into discourse, and as the boundlessness of being underway, without an absolute goal."

2. *Speech*

The next step is more arduous, as the trainer repeatedly jabs the can-opener (the latest phallic weapon) into the victim's buttocks until he begins to speak. The victim's language will soon be like second nature to him, the narrator adds: "il n'a pas encore l'habitude mais il l'aura" (p. 85) / "it's not yet second nature but it will be" (p. 68). It is also at this point that the tormentor keeps the tormented's sack at a distance, depriving him of the loved object.

3. *Script*

The pedagogue then carves letters onto the victim's back with his nail, imprinting his own past and religious beliefs in which he himself has lost faith: "quatre pleins dos de caractères serrés l'enfance la croyance le bleu les miracles tout perdu jamais eu" (p. 87) / "four full backs of close characters the childhood the belief the blue the miracles all lost never was" (p. 70).

4. *The Name*

In this final stage, the trainer marks his own name on the back of his victim, "Toi Pim" / "You Pim," thus successfully completing the process of torturing his creature into a replica of himself, another self which he ultimately reabsorbs.

And finally, the narrator imagines that he is an empty place through which sweeps a voice originating from and returning to "ce pas des nôtres" (p. 167) / "that not one of us" (p. 139), evoking — partly through the sounds of the French words — a transcendental *pater noster*, the Logos, the origin, end, and self-presence of the voice. And that supposition too is withdrawn at the end. No sack, no Pim, no other voice than the narrators' remains, echoing snatches from the polyphony of voices within.

So that after *Comment c'est* Beckett's writing, this fragmentary, discontinuous, but nevertheless astoundingly revealing journey through the psyche, refusing what has been, suffering what is, anticipating what might be, plays in the meanwhile with the human and inhuman and transhuman traces in us all.

CONCLUSION

In *Company* (published in 1980), Beckett recapitulates and comments on the abysmal games of his previous novels to the extent that discussing this fable and *Mal vu mal dit* (published in 1981) permits me both to summarize and extend the foregoing remarks.

Thus, in considering *Company*'s intricate narrative stances, we find a third-person narrator situating his figments in a vaguely defined time and space: someone lying on his back in darkness hears a voice telling of a present, a past, and at times announcing a future. The past predominates, although it is uncertain whose past is being told. And from the start, the reader is amply warned that the narration is unreliable, not to be confused with the truth, for the most part. By the time the reader reaches the third paragraph, however, another voice comments about the narration so far, a metanarrative voice that distinguishes itself from "the voice" and from the third-person narrator termed "that cankerous other" (p. 8), and finally from an only hypothetical first-person narrator. Below therefore the cast up to this point according to the metanarrative commentator:

Speaker	*Spoken to and about*
the voice	you
the third-person narrator	he
(a first-person narrator	I)

All of the above are contained in the metanarrator, who has split into the various narrating/narrated roles, with his identity shifting according to his place in the discourse: he is the voice and "you," the narrator and "he." Only the first person is rejected.

That this self-conscious narrator can use many disguises but not the first person is made clear in different ways by the English and French versions. The former specifies that if the third-person narrator could speak to and about the second-person addressee of the voice, "there would be a first" (p. 8), that is, to the third-person and second-person masks would be added a first-person narrator. The French version, on the other hand, stipulates that in that case there would be a third: "il y aurait une troisième" (p. 9). Punning on the English "person" and the French *personne,* both meaning a pronoun form and an individual, the English original opts for the first meaning (there would be a first-person narrator) and the French translation for the second, i.e., instead of two speakers there would be three.

It is interesting to note in the above context that the term "person" derives from the Latin word *persona,* meaning "mask," which in turn corresponds to the Greek word for "dramatic character" or "role." The terms "first, second, third-person" were applied by grammarians to pronouns on the model of ancient drama in which the leading role was played by the first person, the auxiliary role by the second person, and the remaining roles by the third person on stage. On the basis of this analogy, all discourse is a drama of masks with the first person, on whose point of view all others depend, in starring position.[1] In *Company,* then, Beckett attacks the system of pronouns — the way they function in everyday and narrative discourse — by undermining the first-person or principal role.

Beckett's unmasking of the first person's determining role in discourse can be followed from the first works to the last. The early texts, as we have seen, had without fail let the anonymous third-person narrator's mask slip to show a first person behind it. It would seem, then, that the god-like mask of third-person narrators serves to conceal the even greater god behind it, the narcissistic persona of the creator: the first person and cause of the drama. That in the early works the protagonist confides his secrets to the creator, is co-present with him as an inner voice, served to displace the first person from creator to inner voice,

---

[1] For a discussion of this grammatical "egocentricity," see John Lyons, *Semantics,* II, 638 f.

mask after mask, *ad infinitum.* Then in *Molloy*'s theatre of the mind, we find that the first person plays all three parts: speaker, spoken to, spoken about. And as this fragmentation of the "I" into three repeats itself endlessly, each narrator finally rejects the first person for the third. Malone, embedding third-person stories in his self-narration and vowing near the end to avoid the first person altogether, nevertheless breaks his promise at once. Then, in *L'Innommable*'s all-out assault on pronouns, they are indicted in accordance with three semantic principles. First, according to the principle of non-identity, words are not the things to which they refer; pronouns are but masks: language points to an absence. Secondly, in accordance with the principle of non-allness, no matter how much is said — all the pronouns tried one after the other and together — language cannot fully represent an event or a person: all language is a lie. And thirdly, as stipulated by the linguistic relativity theory, the particular language — or pronoun system — we use determines the way we think: language is a prison.[2] Silence, however, is also out of reach, given that the inner murmurs never cease, so that the writer turns to clowning with words and pronouns, trying them on and off knowing full well they will not fit. For finally, the semantic principle of self-reflexivity — language can be used to comment on language — permits the creative play with words beyond the passive endurance of their limits. Aware of the arbitrary nature of language and of its rules, the writer sabotages the system from within, playfully breaking the rules for the esthetic pleasure of the game.

From *Molloy* on, though, the first person is more bitterly attacked than the other two, for beyond the reasons outlined above, it is its egocentric role in discourse that is being put to question.

---

[2] The principles of "non-identity" and "non-allness," postulated by Alfred Korzybski, are similar to many other theories on the limits of language among which Bertrand Russell's and Fritz Mauthner's. I have used the above terms for their succinctness. On Korzybski's principles and their relation to other semantic theories, see Anatol Rapoport, "What Is Semantics?" *American Scientist* (Jan. 1952); rpt. in *Classics in Semantics,* ed. Donald E. Hayden and E. Paul Alworth (New York: Philosophical Library, 1965), pp. 337-54. For the linguistic relatively theory, see Benjamin Lee Whorf, *Language, Thought and Reality* (1940); rpt. in *Selected Writings of Benjamin Lee Whorf,* ed. John B. Carroll (Cambridge, Mass.: The MIT Press, 1956).

Although *Comment c'est* launches no fresh offensive, many of the short works of the sixties and seventies either side-step the issue by the ellipsis of subject pronouns or, to the contrary, foreground it by the vehement rejection of the first person as in the play *Not I.*

Then, in *Company,* the first person is excised from the narrative, a feat the previous texts only announced. The first person is present — like nothingness and silence — only as what cannot be. Against this backdrop, another peekaboo game is played substituting the second or third person for the absent first. Not in the sense that they could take its place, but as a game on the border of meaninglessness, since meaning is out of reach. As the voice describes it toward the end: "The process continues none the less lapped as it were in its meaninglessness" (p. 61). (The French version translates this into "enrobé pour ainsi dire de son absurdité" [p. 85]).

The game is played as follows. That the voice, hearer, and narrator are all the inventions of another narrator, after being intimated by the third paragraph's metacommentary, is made explicit further on. Again, three narrators of an infinite chain are indicated: "Deviser of the voice and of its hearer and of himself.... He speaks of himself as of another. He says speaking of himself, He speaks of himself as of another" (p. 26). Each self-quoting narrator refers to himself as a narrated "he" instead of "I." One suspects of course that the narrator who uses "he" to talk about the hearer is in that case as well making use of a deviant self-reflexive mode, is "speaking of himself as of another." And furthermore, we learn that were the hearer to refer to himself he would do so in the third person (p. 45). This then could be called infinite self-narration in the guise of psycho-narration, the preferred stance of the early Beckettian narrators. Instead of saying that the character is my other self, or "I am speaking of myself as of another," as did the early narrators (directly or indirectly), the narrators in *Company* point to their role of narrators always narrated by still another narrator by saying of themselves, "He speaks of himself as of another."

It is interesting to note that the substitution of the third for the first-person pronoun in directly quoted and self-quoted speech becomes the rule in Beckettian narrative and drama after *Com-*

CONCLUSION

pany. This deviation from the expected startles in the texts of the early eighties. Thus, in *Rockaby,* the woman on stage murmurs to herself the words which the voice quotes the woman repeating to herself about herself: "time she stopped." And the figure of *Mal vu mal dit,* although only shown once speaking to herself, does so in the third person (p. 14); the narrator too of the latter work refers to himself as to somebody else: "l'autre" (pp. 19-20). The drama of persons is particularly well staged in *Ohio Impromptu,* in which a reader reads a story to a listener. The story is told in the third person about the listener (usually second person) and the reader himself (usually first person), those two fragments of one figure. The reader quoted within the story, however, does use the first person of himself, the second to the listener. It is as if the third-person narration embeds a more archaic first-person version in the manner Winnie in *Happy Days* exclaims "the old style" with the mention of time's passing.

In returning now to *Company*'s play with infinity, it is clear from the foregoing that the text stages a devised deviser devising a devised deviser devising a devised deviser and so on in unending progression. Indeed, in one direction, when one of the narrators wonders where the chain would end, he finds it unthinkable that it would: "Who asks in the end, Who asks?... And adds long after to himself. Unless another still. Nowhere to be found. Nowhere to be sought. The unthinkable last of all. Unnamable. Last person. I" (p. 24). (The pun on last person — final cause — and first-person pronoun underlines the first person's role in discourse.) And in the other direction, the narrator, after having tried the names "H" and "M" on the hearer in vain, decides after each attempt to leave him "Unnamable" (pp. 32, 45). (The narrator makes an equally futile try at naming himself "W.") So that hypothetically there is an ultimate narrator, an unreachable unnamable who would be "I" on one end, and on the other, an unnamable hearer to whom this narrator could say "I," bridging the abyss. Here then the abysmal structure of the novels since *Watt* is made explicit by the metacommentary.

Could the two hypothetical ends coincide in perfect self-proximity (I am who am), the writer could create himself, be both his alpha and omega, the first and the last. That the writer strains in vain to imitate the Creator, mimics repetedly the "conjuring of something out of nothing," as page 53 of *Company* puts it, has been mocked by Beckettian texts from the beginning. The tenacity with which the theme of the writer who in the process of giving birth to himself aborts reoccurs in Beckett's works ("is it better abort than be barren" asks a line of the 1936 poem "Cascando"),[3] leads me to conclude that, as Ehrenzweig indicates, the birthing process is the central myth of artistic creation, a myth Beckett dismantles along with other myths — with some regret it would seem — substituting for it another version of play with infinity. It is as if this myth represents a permanent temptation. "Quick leave him," is the refrain in *Company* whenever the image of the creator surfaces; the French, "Vite motus," is no less urgent. The image of the creator, moreover, is amply parodied by *Company*'s crawling creator/deviser too taken up with his crawling to create (p. 53).

Company's play, then, both a repetition and a variation on the peekaboo game, has one narrator dividing into two third-person masks dividing into two, dividing into two, and so on without ever reaching the impossible "I," first and last, in the sense that one divided by two, divided by two and so on will never reach zero and continued fractions trail on endlessly. And as if the one series were not enough, there is, as we have seen, a parallel one splitting the narrator into voice and hearer.

Furthermore, in *Company*, as in *L'Innommable*, the abysmal game is both infinite and paradoxical, since the final paragraph shows the hearer inventing his inventor: "But with face upturned for good labour in vain at your fable.... The fable of one with you in the dark. The fable of one fabling of one with you in the dark" (pp. 62-63). Like the Unnamable of the novel, this unnamable invents the fable that invents him, is both the unnamable deviser on one end of the chain and the unnamable devised on the other, containing the fable that contains him.

And since devised by the deviser, the voice too, speaking the above words to the hearer is the invention of the hearer who speaks the voice he hears, describes the voice describing him. He

---

[3] The line was later changed to, "is it not better abort than be barren." See Raymond Federman and John Fletcher, *Samuel Beckett: His Works and His Critics* (Berkeley: Univ. of California Press, 1970), p. 20.

CONCLUSION

alone has created the cast "for company," which as in any drama is an illusion, a dramatic company of masks. He has staged this inner mirror drama in the way the abandoned child plays with the glass, fracturing his image into an infinite company who address each other in the second and third person to mask the absence of the first.

Let us now examine more closely the fiction of the voice and its hearer. First, it would seem that where there is a "you" there must be an "I," that by definition there is no second person without a first. This, however, is what the Beckettian attack on pronouns would contest. Thus, were the voice to speak of itself it would do so in the third person — as someone absent or offstage — as do the other members of *Company*. Unlike the third-person mask, however, the second-person disguise is relatively recent in Beckett's writing, its most memorable instances before *Company* being the 1965 *Imagination morte imaginez* / *Imagination Dead Imagine* and the 1976 play *That Time,* in which the listener hears his own voices A B C recount his past in the second person. In *Imagination morte imaginez,* although the narrator addresses the commands to himself, the second-person plural form, in which the orders are cast, appears to involve the reader in a manner reminiscent of Michel Butor's use of *vous* in his 1957 novel *La Modification.*[4] But whereas Beckett's use of *vous* above is a type of metacommentary, Butor was experimenting with self-narration in the second person plural. Beckett, then, added this deviant narrative stance to his repertoire in *That Time* and *Company,* substituting the singular *tu* for *vous,* and as an added complication, embedding this pose in *Company* into an equally anomalous third-person self-narration.

Company's voice tells the hearer his life story of which fifteen segments are given stretching from birth to present situation (near death). Within the work this span is expressed in terms of light and dark: from when he first saw the light to near darkness. Each vignette takes the form of a story told to and about the hearer, somewhat in the manner parents tell children about their birth

---

[4] *La Modification* (Paris: Minuit, 1957). *A Change of Heart,* trans. Jean Stewart (New York: Simon and Schuster, 1959).

and early childhood. (Indeed, at one point, the voice — "No trace of love" — is compared to that of a mother and father murmuring to a newborn [p. 47]). And although the voice is made to speak in flat tones, each biographical fragment is impeccably composed with an ear for esthetic patterns and in accordance with conventions of narrative fiction. The stories have an orientation (situating the characters in a time and place; vague as these might be for the reader, they are obviously not so for the hearer), usually followed by a narrative sequence consisting of a complicating action and resolution, and finally a closing routine or coda which may be an evaluation or a circling back from the time of the narrative toward the narrator's present.[5] The first story (already familiar from *Comment c'est*), approximately one page in length, can serve as an illustration:

> *Orientation:* "A small boy you come out of Connolloy's Stores holding your mother by the hand. You turn right.... It is late afternoon..." (p. 10).
>
> *Complicating Action:* The boy asks his mother twice whether the sky in reality is more distant than it appears.
>
> *Resolution:* The mother, refusing to answer, shakes off the boy's hand and makes a cutting remark.
>
> *Coda:* The question must have angered her. He has never forgotten the insult.

The use of the narrative present tense in the biographical fragments (except for the birth narrative, embedded flashbacks, and occasional lapses into the past) points to the peculiar status of the stories as transcriptions of memory traces, of texts embedded in the archives of the mind far removed from what took place. There are frequent indications of how the hearer sees the scene now as compared to then, in the sense parents will ask a child, "you do

---

[5] This description of narrative sequencing comes from Elizabeth Closs Traugott and Mary Louise Pratt, *Linguistics for Students of Literature* (New York: Harcourt Brace Jovanovich, 1980), Chapter 6. Traugott and Pratt in turn based their discussion of narrative on the approach developed in William Labov, *Language in the Inner City* (Philadelphia: Univ. of Pennsylvania Press, 1972), Chapter 9.

remember, don't you?" However, since the birth story focuses on the father's activities during the hours preceding the birth of the son, this segment cannot but have the status of a story from the beginning and is consequently told in the narrative past. Birth itself, of course, engraves itself indelibly into the mind. Certainly not, though, in the classical narrative sense: I was born on such and such a day at such and such a time in such and such a place, and so on, although children often confuse such details taken from others with their memories. To the contrary, birth's history is translated into the language of dreams and the inner drama of the mind. This inner biography, then is not the story the voice tells, for *Company*'s biographical material is what is readily available to conscious recall and shares the status of the images in *Krapp's Last Tape, Comment c'est, Film,* and other works, that is, it consists of reproductions of a past partly identifiable with the author's biography, partly not, of a fictionalized past from which the writer takes his distance. When one considers the secondary nature of these biographical sketches, in that they are the rewriting of memory inscriptions (and/or other stories), which in turn are fragmentary recordings of events only partially perceived and perceivable, then one may well say that *Company* ridicules the pretension of biographical writing to knowledge about its subject. This theme, familiar from *Watt* on, is succinctly formulated in the following phrase from *Mal vu mal dit:* "La tête trahit les traîtres yeux et le traître mot leurs trahisons" (p. 61).[6] Thus, just as earlier texts posited a dissonance between the writer and his first and third-person stand-ins, these fragments do so between him and the second-person figment. The writer is not found there. He is only as it were spinning his yarns on the border of the abyss.

This is not to say that Beckett could not do any biographer one better about the major themes of his life; this he has done throughout his writing and does again in *Company* perhaps as an exquisite exercise in futility, recording another pseudo-life among the many he has written, or perhaps as an enjoyable game, in the way he invigorates mythical categories before they are undone.

---

[6] Since, as this book goes to press, no English translation is available, I translate as follows: "The mind betrays the traitorous eyes and the traitorous word their traitor."

One must remember, though, that ultimately these exercises are framed as labyrinthine mind games, a process "lapped as it were in its meaninglessness."

On the narrative level, however, when they are taken for what they are there, namely stories to keep the hearer company, to hide his aloneness, the fifteen fragments appear closely related in theme to the third-person narrative. A quick synopsis of the stories will help show how. (The synopsis is in the third person, whereas the narratives, it must be remembered, are in the second.)

Segment	Synopsis	Pages
1	On a late summer afternoon, as a small boy, he is reprimanded by his mother for asking questions about the distance of the sky.	10-11
2	To avoid the unpleasant aspects of birth, his father walked all day in the mountains, then waited in the garage, until the son's birth at nightfall.	12-14
3	As the end of a day of walking, as an old man, accompanied by his father's shade, he stops on a country road to count his steps and add the day's total to that of previous days.	14-15
4	On returning from kindergarten, he opens a garden gate for an old beggar woman who blesses him for it. The woman within the house, deaf and out of her mind, believing she could fly, had thrown herself one day from her first floor window.	16-17
5	At the tip of a high board above the sea, he looks down to the face of his father urging him to jump.	18
6	Alone in the garden at tea time, he repeatedly throws himself from a great fir, the branches breaking his fall. He hears his mother tell a visitor that he has misbehaved.	21-22
7	At nightfall, on the Ballyogan Road, in the company of his father's shade, he counts	23-24

CONCLUSION 143

Segment	Synopsis	Pages
	his steps. His coat, boots, and hat are briefly described.	
8	At daybreak, he climbs to a hiding place in the hills to glimpse a distant mountain. Others ridiculed him when he told of seing it from there. From then on, he keeps it to himself.	25
9	One autumn afternoon in the garden, he places a hedgehog in a hutch enclosed in a hatbox to protect it from the cold. The good feeling he enjoys at the thought of his good deed soon gives way to misgivings. When he could make himself look in the hutch, he found the decomposed body. (Last half told in the narrative past.)	29-31
10	During his last outing, one spring, he walks through pastures covered with snow and lambs and scattered red placentae. Following the path he always takes, no longer accompanied by his father's shade, no longer counting steps, since each day they average the same, he suddenly stops halfway through the pasture unable to go on.	35-38
11	As a young man, in May, he is joined by a woman in a little summerhouse. The narrator embeds a flashback of the young boy imitating his father's chuckle as he read *Punch* there on Sunday afternoons. As he now waits for the woman, he does a number of mental calculations, as these are a help to him in time of trouble. When she appears, he thinks she might be pregnant, the size of her abdomen evoking his father's after Sunday lunch. The couple sit face to face, each sunk in their own mind.	38-42
12	In the shade of an aspen, with an unnamed woman, eyes in each other's eyes, their faces hidden by her hair, he listens to the leaves.	47-48

Segment	Synopsis	Pages
13	Leaning on a long staff at evening in the dying light, his back to the sea, he hears it ebb and flow. The shadow of the staff on the sand vanishes last.	54
14	He spends a sleepless night thinking of the woes of humanity. At one point, he turns on the light and studies the rotations of a watch's second hand and calculates the waxing and waning of its shadow. Then till dawn he returns to humanity's woes until his shadow and those of other objects appear with the rising sun.	57-59
15	After he could go out no longer, he sat huddled in Belacqua's pose in a dark windowless place. He imagines in vain the fable that he is not alone. After alternating for a time between the fetal and supine positions, he is now on his back for good continuing his fable nearing its end. The last word he hears is "alone."	60-63

Repetition, circularity, and solitary play are some of the major elements of this pseudo-biographical series as well as the semantic oppositions near/far, inside/outside, male/female, light/dark, motion/stasis, birth/death. Many of the fragments contain mental calculations of distance, an activity segment 11 stipulates has always helped in time of trouble. However, after the question about how far away the sky (no. 1) and his sighting a distant mountain (no. 8) are met with ridicule, he learns to keep silent about such matters.

An intriguing association of pseudo-events begins with segment 2 in which the father wanders away from home, keeping his distance, and finally waits in the garage until the son's birth is "over." (There is insistence on the word "over" in the text.) The segment immediately following and numbers 7, 10, 13, and 15 tell of the son as an old man repeating his father's wanderings, counting his steps to himself and figuring the distance until his birth is almost "over" in a sense, until he is near death. And since he translates the distance covered into how many times he has circled the globe, the repeated to and fro along the same road is bent into a circle. This solitary wanderer, for a time accompanied by his father's shade, resembles Beckett's persona in the post-war novels and *Godot*: the same coat, boots, and hat; the counting games; the going in circles on a country road in twilight; and finally while awaiting death or birth in a womb and tomb-like place, imagining what preceded, making figments come and go for company, playing with infinity. This persona, then, is as much part of the writer's pseudo-life as the childhood and young manhood memories and as false.

Several other stories speak of the child imitating the father. In number 11, that he tries to chuckle like his father reading *Punch* in the summerhouse pleases the father greatly. When much later, suspecting that his lover is pregnant, he associates her abdomen with the father's bulging stomach, this image of a uterine father brings to mind *Molloy*. It is as if the son in becoming a father like his father at the same time projects a mother identity onto the father he is imitating, blending the two opposites into one.

Nor is the image of the bad as compared to the good father missing. Another series of associations informs segments 4 to 6, in each of which figures a jump from an unusual height. The fifth story is perhaps the most unfinished of all the sketches: the complicating action in remaining unresolved takes on the status of a moment of terror frozen in time. The situation of the child on the high board seeing his father's "loved trusted face" (p. 18) mirrored in the sea, feeling his and the crowd's eyes on him, and hearing his father's call to be brave and jump, suggests a double bind. He loves/trusts his father, yet one intimates that the terror makes him mistrust/hate him. Since the following segment tells of the boy repeatedly hurling himself off a tree in the garden and the one preceding of a deaf woman "not in her right mind" (p. 16) jumping from a window in the belief she could fly, one might take it that the child repeats the traumatic moment on the high board in play in order to prove to himself the impossible, that is, that he wants to jump, is brave, does voluntarily what the father forced him to do. That it might also be a way of punishing his parents, frightening them as they frightened him, is intimated by the mother's words to a visitor while he is tree diving in the garden: "He has been a very naughty boy" (p. 22). An interpretation just as likely, though, is that the child seeks out the exhiliration which the moment of danger and panic on the board had made known to him, that instead of playing to master his fear, he plays for the thrill children discover in such vertigo-inducing games.[7] What the above three suppositions suggest, moreover, is that interpreting such biographical tidbits also resembles juggling with meaning on the edge of a bottomless pit of possible explanations.

The mother is mentioned in relation to the son only in the first and sixth stories in both of which she disapproves of him. But she may also be said to play an indirect role in several other pieces, such as the fourth and the ninth, which are closely linked thematically. In these the child takes the role of protector, opening the gate for the beggar woman in one, a kindness for which he is blessed by her, and in the other, providing warmth, shelter, and food for the hedgehog he meets while playing alone in the garden. In the latter instance, he pities the animal mistakenly, indeed for his not its own good, thus causing the creature's death. Pity then is an ambiguous force, praiseworthy in the first instance, in which the child helps the woman do what she wants to do, self-serving and deadly in the second. The dual role of enclosure too, positive and negative, life and death-giving, is a familiar theme from the novels and the fictional series of *Company* which stage the paradox of an exteriority striving for an interiority which is a vain attempt

---

[7] The first two explanations are based on Freud's repetition compulsion in *Beyond the Pleasure Principle* and the Kleinian theory of repression according to which painful experiences are inverted to pleasurable ones. See my discussion of the *fort/da* game in Part II. The third possibility comes from Roger Caillois, who gives the following interpretation of such vertiginous games in *Les Jeux et les hommes: Le Masque et le vertige*, 2nd ed. (Paris: Gallimard, Idées, 1967), pp. 324-25: "Certes, le vertige suppose la peur, plus précisément un sentiment panique, mais ce dernier attire, fascine: il est un plaisir. Il s'agit moins de triompher de la peur, que d'éprouver voluptueusement une peur, un frisson, une stupeur qui font perdre momentanément le contrôle de soi." The English translation, *Man, Play, and Games*, trans. Meyer Barash (New York: Free Press of Glencoe, 1961), p. 169, reads as follows: "To be sure, vertigo presupposes fear or, more precisely, feelings of panic, but the latter attracts and fascinates one; it is pleasurable. It is not so much a question of triumphing over fear as of the voluptuous experience of fear, thrills, and shock that causes a momentary loss of self-control."

to recapture an exteriority striving for an interiority and so forth, thus blurring this pair of opposites along with the others.

Although in most of the stories the child or man is alone, playing, wandering, and calculating on his own (no other children enter into these scenes and father and mother only intermittently), segments 11 and 12 stage meeting with two different women. In the former fragment, the young man and woman sit face to face without looking at each other, each enclosed within him/herself. In the latter, in poignant contrast, he looks into the woman's eyes looking into his, for once abolishing distance and the desire for play. As one might recall, *Krapp's Last Tape* and *Words and Music* had evoked a similar idyllic moment from the past.

Finally, the concluding segments (11 through 15) focus insistently on the images of repetition and circularity introduced in earlier stories and so apparent in *Company*'s narrative structure. Thus, fragment 11 speaks of calculating the number of heartbeats of a lifetime, the pulsating rhythm of the body's circulation, followed in segment 12 by the old man listening to the sea's ebb and flow, whereas in number 14, the "you" as young man calculates the waxing and waning of the shadow of his watch's second hand until the morning sun casts shadows around his room. These scenes thus effectively associate biological, human, and cosmic rhythms. The coming and going of blood, of the sea, of light and dark, of steps in the shadow of time are turned into an infinite round which the games with infinity played by the fabling narrator repeat. Against this circular motion, however, are set moments of stasis and a linear progression leading to the nearly motionless body on its back alone in the timeless dark on the edge of death or birth.

Whereas the stories told in *Company* are a blend of biographical and fictional material, which the narrator split into voice and hearer tells himself and embeds in an unending narrative chain, the single narrator of *Mal vu mal dit* speaks (badly) of what the eye glimpses (badly) of an inner drama. (As already mentioned, the third person is used throughout both for the unnamed female figure and for the narrator.) Whether the narrator is speaking of a real or an imagined scene is indifferent since as he writes, the two blend into each other and one is as much a lie as the other (pp. 49-50). For, as the title announces, the familiar refrain of the inadequacy of perception and language is sounded throughout the text. What we read in *Mal vu mal dit,* then, is not only another transcription, faulty and partial as the others, of an inner text, but we witness again the narrator's attempt to free himself from the illusory traces within.

In *Mal vu mal dit,* of all the traces the most indelible is that of the maternal figure. As such this figure is a pendant to the father's shade in *Company* which long accompanies the wanderer before disappearing. And as in earlier works, mythological, biblical, and autobiographical details intermingle to suggest the author's mother, the mother of Christ, and a cosmic divinity. Her image here, however, is mostly that of a *mater dolorosa* whose realm suggests a hibernal version of Lousse's paradise/inferno in *Molloy.* The narrator makes this illusion come and go with the hope of tearing himself away from these powerful inner inscriptions: "Encore faut-il le pouvoir. Pouvoir s'arracher aux traces. De l'illusion" (p. 75).[8]

If as in *Molloy, Mal vu mal dit* attempts to transcribe into words a vision deeply embedded in the psyche, the mythic realm of the mother (in the Jungian sense), then it is interesting to note how this text compares with that of some thirty years earlier. It is of course not only the inner text which is transformed in time, but the eyes viewing it, as well as the narrator's way of playing with this psychic fragment among many. Since continual changes are noted in the text, the narrator himself questions their how and why and when (pp. 64-66). As suggested by the title, the narrator particularly emphasizes the role of the "traitorous" eye. And since the eye's vision is described in the mythic present tense as if, the narrator specifies, the woman were still alive (p. 8), words as always betray what is already a betrayal.

In *Mal vu mal dit,* then, the maternal realm maintains the circularity of Lousse's garden and its male attendants (in this instance an apostolic or perhaps zodiacal twelve), its mysterious tomb, its moon and symbolic silver object. The latter, instead of a cruciform knife-rest is a pisciform button-hook hanging from a nail. Like the two Xs of the knife-rest, the fish shape is rich in

---

[8] "First one has to be able to do so. Able to wrench free from the traces. Of illusion." (My translation.)

associations, bringing to mind Pisces, the twelfth sign of the zodiac coinciding with the vernal equinox; Cybele, the mother-goddess, attended by young male divinities, who through her love drove Attis, her son and consort, to madness, castration, and death, and whose worshippers venerated the fish;[9] and Christ's sacrifice to which the text makes specific reference: the nail attaching the button-hook evokes the crucifying nails on Calvary (p. 72).

Unlike Lousse's multi-colored flower garden, however, *Mal vu mal dit*'s landscape with its three parts — a hut situated in the nonexistent center of a circular area of stones which is in turn enveloped by fields (p. 9) — is rapidly turning into snow and stone. Such wintry desolation suggests a number of figures: Demeter (whose name means "earth-mother") grieving the loss of Persephone during a third of the year; the German lunar goddess Frau Holle covering the world with snowflakes; Echo's bones turning to stone; and the icy center of Dante's Inferno, that other journey through the mind's text, the inner book. Most of all, though, the landscape evokes the dying image of the death-bearing mother in the soul. White and black, night and winter, stillness and the immobility of stone, all associated with death, progressively dominate here. Such desolate regions, on death's border, are as we have seen, a part of the artistic process; for Beckett, a part of the writer's repeated come and go to and from the fragments of his open-ended inner text.

Writing, as we have seen in *Watt* and the subsequent novels, entails the process of fraying a path into the embedded archives of the mind consisting of the records of previous frayings and the inscriptions of the past. These psychic inscriptions or inner texts are multi-modal — sound and voice recordings, photographs, films, and scripts — the varied modes of our thought processes and dreams, never original but transcriptions of transcriptions. And as the writer on his path through the psychic archives comes upon the first of the series of embedded records and begins to transcribe it, he notices that he can see and hear it only partially and that it too is full of flaws and gaps through which are noticeable the traces of another text — in the manner of a palimpsest — and in this second layer, he finds the traces of still another and so on to infinity.

---

[9] See Jung, *Symbols of Transformation*, pp. 423-26.

At each stage of the process the records are a mix of real and imaginary memory fragments which are in turn transformed through the transcribing process itself. The writer is thus faced with the task of reconstituting an infinite inner text, of transposing a text at each stage unfathomable and multi-modal into an adequate language. It is not surprising therefore that Beckett has experimented with multi-media productions of all types and within each work has indicted his senses, on the one hand, and language on the other, as unequal to the task of reconstituting the infinite psychic text.

Since language and the other media permit only the illusory communication of an illusion, the Beckettian narrator, who would prefer nothingness to writing, who is oblidged to write without being able to write, has taken several paths. On the one hand, he has made his impotence in the face of this double bind the subject of his writing, and on the other, he has labeled his writing only a game. In this sense he may be compared to a child whose toy (which is already the symbolic substitute for a lost unity) has broken into countless fragments. The child, lamenting the loss of his toy, repeats the shattering moment by the game of lost and found, come and go: he takes a fragment or two and makes them appear and disappear in an endless to and fro. Or, given the impossible task of fitting the pieces back together, he discovers that the fragments can be arranged in an infinite number of ways for his pleasure, and thus losing sight for a moment of the task of reconstituting the lost object or of searching for a super glue, he enjoys the play with shapes, colors, lines, and textures. With his mind as toy, the writer likewise has found a way of writing without writing, a paradoxical way of writing, by turning it into self-reflexive play with infinity.

Privileging the *fort/da* game as so many texts before it, *Mal vu mal dit* thus ends with its vision fading away, with a stage cleared of its illusion. And as three decades earlier in *Malone meurt,* the fade-out coincides with the impossible moment in which birth and death would blend into each other, here described as an arrival's departure, of a first last second: "départ de l'arrivée. Première dernière seconde" (p. 75). In this case too, the moment would be shared by narrated and narrator, by mother and son, since the life that is coming to an end is said to be hers as well as his:

"C'est la vie qui finit. La sienne à elle. La sienne à l'autre" (p. 19).[10] And, again, as in "The Vulture," this imaginary life/death moment would be preceded by the mind devouring its own tissue of illusions and rejoicing in its emptyness (p. 76). *Mal vu mal dit* thus brings to mind the pleasure principle — the triumph of inorganic stillness, all excitations, outer and inner, hushed — which hovers on the horizon of Beckettian texts. For finally, rather than scribble badly about inner traces, the writer would prefer emptiness and silence. Denied this pleasure, he substitutes its closest approximation, the pleasure of abysmal play with the fragments of illusion within.

---

[10] "Life is coming to an end. Hers. The other's." (My translation.)

BIBLIOGRAPHY

Works by Beckett Cited in the Text

Years of first publication if different from the editions cited are given in parenthesis following the titles. Translations into English are separated from the original French works by a slash. All translations by Beckett unless otherwise indicated.

"Assumption." *transition* [Paris], Nos. 16-17 (June 1929), pp. 268-71.
Proust. 1931; rpt. New York: Grove Press, Evergreen [1957].
"Dream of Fair to Middling Women." Written in 1932. Unpublished. Cited in part in *The Novels of Samuel Beckett.* By John Fletcher. London: Chatto and Windus, 1964; and in *Samuel Beckett: Poet and Critic.* By Lawrence E. Harvey. Princeton: Princeton Univ. Press, 1970.
"Dante and the Lobster." *This Quarter* [Paris], 5 (December 1932), 222-36. Rev. version in *More Pricks than Kicks.*
More Pricks than Kicks (1934). New York: Grove Press, 1970.
Rev. of *Poems,* by Rainer Maria Rilke. *The Criterion* [London], 13 (July 1934), 705-07.
Echo's Bones (1935). In *Collected Poems in English and French.* New York: Grove Press, Evergreen, 1977.
Letter to Thomas McGreevy. 10 March 1935. Cited in part in *Samuel Beckett: A Biography.* By Deirdre Bair. New York: Harcourt Brace Jovanovich, 1978, p. 198.
Letter to Thomas McGreevy. 17 July 1936. Cited in part in *Samuel Beckett: A Biography,* pp. 228-29.
Letter To George Reavey. 13 November 1936. Cited in part in *Samuel Beckett: A Biography,* p. 243.
"Cascando" (1936). In *Collected Poems in English and French.* (See edition above.)
Murphy. 1938; rpt. New York: Grove Press, 1957.
"La Fin" (The first part of the story entitled "Suite" published in 1946). Rev. version in *Nouvelles et "Textes pour rien"* (1955). 2nd ed. with 6 illustrations by Avigdor Arikha. Paris: Minuit, 1958. / "The End" (1954). Trans. Richard Seaver in collaboration with the author. In *Stories and "Texts for Nothing"* (1967). New York: Grove Press, Evergreen, 1968.
"L'Expulsé" (1946-47). Rev. version in *Nouvelles et "Textes pour rien"* (Same edition as above.)/"The Expelled" (1962). Trans. Richard Seaver in collaboration with the author. In *Stories and "Texts for Nothing"* (See above.)

BIBLIOGRAPHY

"Peintres de l'empêchement." *Derrière le Miroir*, Nos. 11 and 12 (June 1948), pp. 3, 4, 7.
Molloy. Paris: Minuit, 1951. / *Molloy* (1955). Trans. Patrick Bowles in collaboration with the author. In *Three Novels*. New York: Grove Press, Evergreen Black Cat, 1965.
Malone meurt. Paris: Minuit, 1951. / *Malone Dies* (1956). In *Three Novels*. (See above.)
En attendant Godot. Paris: Minuit, 1952. / *Waiting for Godot*. New York: Grove Press, Evergreen, 1954.
Watt (1953). New York: Grove Press, Evergreen, 1959.
L'Innommable. Paris: Minuit, 1953. / *The Unnamable* (1958). In *Three Novels*. (See above.)
Textes pour rien. In *Nouvelles et "Textes pour rien"* (1955). (See edition above.) / *Texts for Nothing*. In *Stories and "Texts for Nothing"* (1967). (See edition above.)
From an Abandoned Work (1956). In *"First Love" and Other Shorts*. New York: Grove Press, Evergreen, 1974.
Fin de partie. Suivi de "Acte sans paroles I." Paris: Minuit, 1957. / *Endgame. Followed by "Act Without Words."* New York: Grove Press, Evergreen, 1958.
Krapp's Last Tape (1958). In *"Krapp's Last Tape" and Other Dramatic Pieces*. New York: Grove Press, Evergreen, 1960.
Comment c'est. Paris: Minuit, 1961. / *How It Is*. New York: Grove Press, Evergreen, 1964.
Happy Days. New York: Grove Press, Evergreen 1961.
Words and Music (1962). In *"Cascando" and Other Short Dramatic Pieces*. New York: Grove Press, Evergreen, 1968?
Play (1964). In *"Cascando" and Other Short Dramatic Pieces*. (See above.)
Imagination morte imaginez (1965). In *Têtes-mortes*. Paris: Minuit, 1967. / *Imagination Dead Imagine* (1965). In *"First Love" and Other Shorts*. (See edition above.)
Bing. Paris: Minuit, 1966. / *Ping* (1967). In *"First Love" and Other Shorts*. (See edition above.)
Film: Complete Scenario (1967), *Illustrations, Production Shots*. New York: Grove Press, Evergreen, 1969.
Sans. Paris: Minuit, 1969. / *Lessness*. London: Calder and Boyars, 1970.
Mercier et Camier. Paris: Minuit, 1970. / *Mercier and Camier* (1974). New York: Grove Press, Evergreen, 1975.
Le Dépeupleur. Paris: Minuit, 1970. / *The Lost Ones*. New York: Grove Press, Evergreen, 1972.
Not I (1973). In *Ends and Odds: Eight New Dramatic Pieces*. New York: Grove Press, Evergreen, 1976.
That Time. In *Ends and Odds: Eight New Dramatic Pieces*. (See edition above.)
Pour finir encore et autres foirades. Paris: Minuit, 1976. / *Fizzles*. New York: Grove Press, Evergreen, 1976.
"Roundelay." In *Collected Poems in English and French*. (See edition above.)
Company. New York: Grove Press, 1980. / *Compagnie*. Paris: Minuit, 1980.
Rockaby. In *"Rockaby" and Other Short Pieces*. New York: Grove Press, Evergreen, 1981.

Ohio Impromptu. In *"Rockaby" and Other Short Pieces.* (See edition above.)
Mal vu mal dit. Paris: Minuit, 1981.

WORKS ABOUT BECKETT

This list includes books and collections of critical essays consulted and a selection of the articles, mostly on Beckett's fiction, that I have cited or found of particular interest.

Abbott, H. Porter. *The Fiction of Samuel Beckett: Form and Effect.* Berkeley: Univ. of California Press, 1973.
Álvarez, A. *Samuel Beckett.* New York: Viking Press, 1973.
Bair, Deirdre. *Samuel Beckett: A Biography.* New York: Harcourt Brace Jovanovich, 1978.
Barge, Laura. "'Coloured Images' in the 'Black Dark': Samuel Beckett's Later Fiction." *PMLA,* 92 (1977), 273-84.
Barnard, Guy Christian. *Samuel Beckett: A New Approach.* New York: Dodd, Mead, 1970.
Barrett, William. "How I Understand Less and Less Every Year...". *Columbia University Forum,* 2 (Winter 1959), 44-48.
Bataille, Georges. "Le Silence de *Molloy.*" *Critique,* 7 (1951), 387-96.
Ben-Zvi, Linda. "Samuel Beckett, Fritz Mauthner, and the Limits of Language." *PMLA,* 95 (1980), 183-200.
Bernal, Olga. *Langage et fiction dans le roman de Beckett.* Paris: Gallimard, 1969.
Bersani, Leo. *Balzac to Beckett: Center and Circumference in French Fiction.* New York: Oxford Univ. Press, 1970.
Bishop, Tom, and Raymond Federman, eds. *Cahier Samuel Beckett.* *L'Herne,* No. 31 (1976).
Blanchot, Maurice. "Où maintenant? Qui maintenant?" *Nouvelle Nouvelle Revue Française,* 1 (1953), 678-86. / "What Now? Who Now?" Trans. Richard Howard. *Evergreen Review,* 2 (Winter 1959), 222-29.
Boulais, Véronique. "Samuel Beckett: Une écriture en mal de je." *Poétique,* No. 17 (1974), pp. 114-32.
Bowles, Patrick. "How Samuel Beckett Sees the Universe." *The Listener,* 59 (19 June 1958), 1011-12.
Brater, Enoch, ed. Beckett Issue. *Journal of Modern Literature,* 6 (February 1977).
Brooke-Rose, Christine. "Samuel Beckett and the Anti-Novel." *London Magazine,* 5 (December 1958), 38-46.
Calder, John, ed. *Beckett at Sixty: A Festschrift.* London: Calder and Boyars, 1967.
Chadwick, C. "*Waiting for Godot:* A Logical Approach." *Symposium,* 14 (1960), 252-57.
Chalker, John. "The Satiric Shape of *Watt.*" In *Beckett the Shape Changer: A Symposium.* Ed. Katharine Worth. Boston: Routledge and Kegan Paul, 1975, pp. 19-37.
Chevigny, Bell Gale, ed. *Twentieth Century Interpretations of "Endgame."* Englewood Cliffs, N.J.: Prentice-Hall, 1969.

Cmarada, Geraldine. "*Malone Dies:* A Round of Consciousness." *Symposium,* 14 (1960), 199-212.
Coe, Richard N. *Beckett.* London: Oliver and Boyd, 1964.
Cohn, Ruby, ed. Samuel Beckett Issue. *Perspective,* 11 (Autumn 1959).
——. *Samuel Beckett: The Comic Gamut.* New Brunswick, N.J.: Rutgers Univ. Press, 1962.
——, ed. *Casebook on "Waiting for Godot."* New York: Grove Press, 1967.
——. *Back to Beckett.* Princeton: Princeton Univ. Press, 1973.
Cornwell, Ethel F. "Samuel Beckett: The Flight from Self." *PMLA,* 88 (1973), 41-51.
Cousineau, Thomas J. "*Watt:* Language as Interdiction and Consolation." *Journal of Beckett Studies,* No. 4 (Spring 1979), pp. 1-13.
Croussy, Guy. *Beckett.* Paris: Hachette, 1971.
Dearlove, Judith. "The Voice and Its Words: How It Is in Beckett's Canon." *Journal of Beckett Studies,* No. 3 (Summer 1978), pp. 56-75.
Delye, Huguette. *Samuel Beckett ou la philosophie de l'absurde.* Aix-en-Provence: Pensée Universitaire, 1960.
Doherty, Francis. *Samuel Beckett.* London: Hutchinson, 1971.
Driver, Tom F. "Beckett by the Madeleine." *Columbia University Forum,* 4 (Summer 1961), 21-25.
Durozoi, Gérard. *Beckett.* Paris: Bordas, 1972.
Egebak, Niels. *L'Écriture de Samuel Beckett: Contribution à l'analyse sémiotique de textes littéraires contemporains.* Copenhagen: Akademisk Forlag, 1973.
Erickson, John D. "Objects and Systems in the Novels of Samuel Beckett." *L'Esprit Créateur,* 7 (Summer 1967), 113-22.
——, ed. Beckett Issue. *L'Esprit Créateur,* 11 (Fall 1971).
Esslin, Martin, ed. *Samuel Beckett: A Collection of Critical Essays.* Englewood Cliffs, N.J.: Prentice-Hall, 1965.
Federman, Raymond. *Journey to Chaos: Samuel Beckett's Early Fiction.* Berkeley: Univ. of California Press, 1965.
——, and John Fletcher, *Samuel Beckett: His Works and His Critics.* Berkeley: Univ. of California Press, 1970.
——. "The Impossibility of Saying the Same Old Thing the Same Old Way — Samuel Beckett's Fiction since *Comment c'est.*" *L'Esprit Créateur,* 11 (Fall 1971), 21-43.
——. "Samuel Beckett: The Liar's Paradox." In *Samuel Beckett: The Art of Rhetoric.* Ed. Eduoard Morot-Sir, et al. Chapel Hill: North Carolina Studies in the Romance Languages and Literatures, 1976, pp. 119-41.
Finney, Brian H. *Since "How It Is:" A Study of Samuel Beckett's Later Fiction.* London: Covent Garden Press, 1972.
Fitch, Brian T. *Dimensions, structures et textualité dans la trilogie romanesque de Beckett.* Paris: Minard, 1977.
Fletcher, John. "Beckett's Verse: Influences and Parallels." *French Review,* 37 (1964), 320-31.
——. *The Novels of Samuel Beckett.* London: Chatto and Windus, 1964.
——. *Samuel Beckett's Art.* London: Chatto and Windus, 1967.
——, and John Spurling. *Beckett: A Study of His Plays.* New York: Hill and Wang, 1972.

Fournier, Edith. "Pour que la boue me soit contée...". *Critique*, No. 168 (1961), pp. 412-18.
Friedman, Melvin J., ed. *Configuration Critique de Samuel Beckett*. Paris: Minard, 1964. / *Samuel Beckett Now: Critical Approaches to His Novels, Poetry, and Plays*. Chicago: Univ. of Chicago Press, 1970.
Frye, Northrop. "The Nightmare Life in Death." *Hudson Review*, 13 (1960), 442-49.
Garzilli, Enrico. *Circles without Center: Paths to the Discovery and Creation of Self in Modern Literature*. Cambridge: Harvard Univ. Press, 1972.
Gebhardt, Richard C. "Technique of Alienation in *Molloy*." *Perspectives on Contemporary Literature*, 1, No. 2 (1975), 74-84.
Gessner, Niklaus. *Die Unzulänglichkeit der Sprache: Eine Untersuchung über Formzerfall und Beziehungslosigkeit bei Samuel Beckett*. Zürich: Juris-Verlag, 1957.
Gresset, Michel. "Création et cruauté chez Beckett." *Tel Quel*, No. 15 (Autumn 1963), pp. 58-65.
Hamilton, Alice and Kenneth. *Condemned to Life: The World of Samuel Beckett*. Grand Rapids, Mich.: William B. Eerdmans, 1976.
Harrison, Robert. *Samuel Beckett's "Murphy:" A Critical Excursion*. Athens: Univ. of Georgia Press, 1968.
Harvey, Lawrence E. "Samuel Beckett: Initiation du poète." In *Configuration Critique de Samuel Beckett*. Ed. Melvin J. Friedman. Paris: Minard, 1964, pp. 153-68. Rpt., in English, in *Samuel Beckett Now*. Ed. Melvin J. Friedman. Chicago: Univ. of Chicago Press, 1970, pp. 171-84.
―――. *Samuel Beckett: Poet and Critic*. Princeton: Princeton Univ. Press, 1970.
Hassan, Ihab. *The Literature of Silence: Henry Miller and Samuel Beckett*. New York: Alfred A. Knopf, 1967.
Hayman, David. "Quest for Meaninglessness: The Boundless Poverty of Molloy." In *Six Contemporary Novels: Introductory Essays in Modern Fiction*. Ed. William O. S. Sutherland. Austin: Univ. of Texas, 1962, pp. 90-112. Rpt., in French, in *Configuration Critique de Samuel Beckett*. Ed. Melvin J. Friedman. Paris: Minard, 1964, pp. 131-51. Rpt., in English, in *Samuel Beckett Now*. Ed. Melvin J. Friedman. Chicago: Univ. of Chicago Press, 1970, pp. 129-56.
Hesla, David H. "The Shape of Chaos: A Reading of Beckett's *Watt*." *Critique: Studies in Modern Fiction*, 6 (Spring 1963), 85-105.
―――. *The Shape of Chaos: An Interpretation of the Art of Samuel Beckett*. Minneapolis: Univ. of Minnesota Press, 1971.
Hesse, Eva. "Die Welt des Samuel Beckett: Versuch einer Koordinierung." *Akzente*, No. 3 (June 1961), pp. 244-66.
Hoefer, Jacqueline. "*Watt*." *Perspective*, 11 (Autumn 1959), 166-82. Rpt. in *Samuel Beckett: A Collection of Critical Essays*. Ed. Martin Esslin. Englewood Cliffs, N.J.: Prentice-Hall, 1965, pp. 62-76.
Hoffman, Frederick J. *Samuel Beckett: The Language of Self*. 1962; rpt. New York: E. P. Dutton, 1964.
Hokenson, Jan. "A Stuttering Logos: Biblical Paradigms in Beckett's Trilogy." *James Joyce Quarterly*, 8 (1971), 293-310.
Iser, Wolfgang. *The Implied Reader: Patterns of Communication in Prose Fiction from Bunyan to Beckett*. Trans. from the German. Baltimore: Johns Hopkins Press, 1974.

Jacobson, Josephine, and William R. Mueller. *The Testament of Samuel Beckett*. New York: Hill and Wang, 1964.
Janvier, Ludovic. *Pour Samuel Beckett*. Paris: Minuit, 1966.
——. "Le Lieu du retrait de la blancheur de l'écho." *Critique*, No. 237 (1967), pp. 215-38.
——. *Samuel Beckett par lui-même*. Paris: Seuil, 1969.
——. "Lieu dire." *L'Herne*, No. 31 (1976), pp. 193-205.
Karl, Frederick R. "Waiting for Beckett: Quest and Re-Quest." *Sewanee Review*, 69 (1961), 661-76.
Kennedy, Sighle. *Murphy's Bed: A Study of Real Sources and Sur-Real Associations in Samuel Beckett's First Novel*. Lewisburg, Pa.: Bucknell Univ. Press, 1971.
Kenner, Hugh. *Samuel Beckett: A Critical Study*. New York: Grove Press, 1961.
Kern, Edith. "Moran-Molloy: The Hero as Author." *Perspective*, 11 (Autumn 1959), 183-93.
——. "Samuel Beckett — Dionysian Poet." *Descant*, 3 (Winter 1959), 33-36.
——. "Ironic Structure in Beckett's Fiction." *L'Esprit Créateur*, 11 (Fall 1971), 3-13.
——. *Existential Thought and Fictional Technique: Kierkegaard, Sartre, Beckett*. New Haven: Yale Univ. Press, 1970.
Knowlson, James. *Samuel Beckett: An Exhibition*. London: Turret Books, 1971.
——. *Light and Darkness in the Theatre of Samuel Beckett*. London: Turret Books, 1972.
Krance, Charles. "Alienation and Form in Beckett's *How It Is*." *Perspectives on Contemporary Literature*, 1, No. 2 (1975), 85-103.
Krieger, Elliot. "Samuel Beckett's *Texts for Nothing*: Explication and Exposition." *MLN*, 92 (1977), 987-1000.
Kristeva, Julia. "Le Père, l'amour, l'exil." *L'Herne*, No. 31 (1976), pp. 246-52. Rpt. in *Polylogue*. Paris: Seuil, 1977, pp. 137-47.
Law, Richard A. "Mock Evangelism in Beckett's *Watt*." *Modern Language Studies*, 2, No. 2 (1972), 68-82.
Lodge, David. "Some *Ping* Understood." *Encounter*, No. 30 (February 1968), pp. 85-89.
Lyons, Charles R. "Beckett's Major Plays and the Trilogy." *Comparative Drama*, 5 (1971-72), 254-68.
Macksey, Richard. "The Artist in the Labyrinth: Design or *Dasein*." *MLN*, 77 (1962), 239-56.
Marissel, André. *Samuel Beckett*. Classiques du XXe Siècle, 58. Paris: Editions Universitaires, 1963.
Mercier, Vivian. "The Mathematical Limit." *The Nation*, 188 (14 February 1959), 144-45.
——. *Beckett/Beckett*. New York: Oxford Univ. Press, 1977.
Mintz, Samuel I. "Beckett's *Murphy*: A 'Cartesian' Novel." *Perspective*, 11 (Autumn 1959), 156-65.
Montgomery, Niall. "No Symbols Where None Intended." *New World Writing*, No. 5 (April 1954), pp. 324-37.
Mood, John J. " 'The Personal System' — Samuel Beckett's *Watt*." *PMLA*, 86 (1971), 255-65.

Mooney, Michael E. "*Molloy*, Part I: Beckett's *Discourse on Method.*" *Journal of Beckett Studies,* No. 3 (Summer 1978), pp. 40-55.
Moorjani, Angela B. "A Mythic Reading of *Molloy.*" In *Samuel Beckett: The Art of Rhetoric.* Ed. Edouard Morot-Sir, et al. Chapel Hill: North Carolina Studies in the Romance Languages and Literatures, 1976, pp. 225-35.
――――. "Narrative Game Strategies in Beckett's *Watt.*" *L'Esprit Créateur,* 17 (1977), 235-44.
――――. Rev. Article of *Samuel Beckett: A Biography,* by Deirdre Bair. *MLN,* 93 (1978), 1106-15.
――――, and Wolfgang Freese. "The Esoteric and the Trivial: Chess and Go in the Novels of Beckett and Kawabata." *Perspectives on Contemporary Literature,* Lexington: Univ. Press of Kentucky, 1981, pp. 37-48.
Morot-Sir, Edouard, et al., eds. *Samuel Beckett: The Art of Rhetoric.* Chapel Hill: North Carolina Studies in the Romance Languages and Literatures, 1976.
――――. "Samuel Beckett and Cartesian Emblems." In *Samuel Beckett: The Art of Rhetoric,* pp. 25-104.
Nadeau, Maurice. "Samuel Beckett ou le droit au silence." *Temps Modernes,* 7 (1952), 1273-82.
Nores, Dominique, ed. *Les Critiques de notre temps et Beckett.* Paris: Garnier, 1971.
O'Hara, J. D., ed., *Twentieth Century Interpretations of "Molloy," "Malone Dies," "The Unnamable": A Collection of Critical Essays.* Englewood Cliffs, N. J.: Prentice-Hall, 1970.
Onimus, Jean. *Beckett.* Les Ecrivains Devant Dieu, 16. [Paris]: Desclée De Brouwer, 1968.
Perche, Louis. *Beckett: L'Enfer à notre portée.* Paris: Centurion, 1969.
Perlmutter Ruth. "Beckett's *Film* and Beckett and Film." *Journal of Modern Literature,* 6 (February 1977), 83-94.
Pilling, John. *Samuel Beckett.* London: Routledge and Kegan Paul, 1976.
Pingaud, Bernard. Rev. of *Molloy. Esprit,* 19 (1951), 423-25.
――――. "*Molloy* douze ans après." *Les Temps Modernes,* 19 (1963), 1283-1300. Rpt. in *Molloy.* Paris: Union Générale d'Editions, 10/18, 1963, pp. 289-311.
――――. "'Dire, c'est inventer.'" *Quinzaine Littéraire.* No. 67 (February 1969), pp. 5-6.
Pouillon, Jean. Rev. of *Molloy. Les Temps Modernes,* 7 (1951), 184-86.
Rabinovitz, Rubin. "*Watt* from Descartes to Schopenhauer." In *Modern Irish Literature: Essays in Honor of William York Tindall.* Ed. Raymond J. Porter and James D. Brophy. New York: Iona College Press, 1972, pp. 261-87.
――――. "Style and Obscurity in Samuel Beckett's Early Fiction." *Modern Fiction Studies,* 20 (1974), 399-406.
――――. "The Addenda to Samuel Beckett's *Watt.*" In *Samuel Beckett: The Art of Rhetoric.* Ed. Eduard Morot-Sir, et al. Chapel Hill: North Carolina Studies in the Romance Languages and Literatures, 1976, pp. 211-23.
――――. "*Molloy* and the Archetypal Traveller." *Journal of Beckett Studies,* No. 5 (Autumn 1979), pp. 25-44.
Robinson, Michael. *The Long Sonata of the Dead: A Study of Samuel Beckett.* New York: Grove Press, 1969.

Rose, Gilbert J. "On the Shores of Self: Samuel Beckett's *Molloy*-Irredentism and the Creative Impulse." *Psychoanalytic Review*, 60 (1973), 587-604.
Saint-Martin, Fernande. *Samuel Beckett et l'univers de la fiction.* Montréal: Presses de l'Université de Montréal, 1976.
Schneider, Alan. "On Directing *Film.*" In *Film*. By Samuel Beckett. New York: Grove Press, 1969, pp. 63-94.
Schulz, Hans-Joachim. *This Hell of Stories: A Hegelian Approach to the Novels of Samuel Beckett.* The Hague: Mouton, 1973.
Scott, Nathan A. *Samuel Beckett.* London: Bowes and Bowes, 1965.
Senneff, Susan Field. "Song and Music in Samuel Beckett's *Watt.*" *Modern Fiction Studies*, 11 (Summer 1964), 137-49.
Shapiro, Barbara. "Toward a Psychoanalytic Reading of Beckett's *Molloy.*" 2 parts. *Literature and Psychology*, 19 (1969), No. 2, 71-86; Nos. 3 and 4, 15-30.
Sherzer, Dina. "Quelques manifestations du narrateur-créateur dans *Molloy* de Samuel Beckett." *Language and Style*, 5 (1972), 115-22.
———. *Structure de la Trilogie de Beckett.* The Hague: Mouton, 1976.
Skerl, Jennie. "Fritz Mauthner's 'Critique of Language' in Samuel Beckett's *Watt.*" *Contemporary Literature*, 15 (1974), 474-87.
Smith, Stephani Pofahl. "Between Pozzo and Godot: Existence as Dilemma." *French Review*, 47 (1974), 889-903.
———. "From Poetics to Anti-Poetics." In *Samuel Beckett: The Art of Rhetoric.* Ed. Edouard Morot-Sir, et al. Chapel Hill: North Carolina Studies in the Romance Languages and Literatures, 1976, pp. 157-63.
Solomon, Philip H. *The Life after Birth: Imagery in Beckett's Trilogy.* University, Miss.: Romance Monographs, 1975.
Taat, A. Mieke. "Les Signes du feu." *L'Arc*, No. 49 (1972), pp. 78-88.
Tagliaferri, Aldo. *Beckett et la surdétermination littéraire.* Trans. from the Italian by Nicole Fama. Paris: Payot, 1977.
Tindall, William York. *Samuel Beckett.* Columbia Essays on Modern Writers, 4. New York: Columbia Univ. Press, 1964.
Warhaft, Sidney. "Threne and Theme in *Watt.*" *Wisconsin Studies in Contemporary Literature*, 4 (1963), 261-78.
Webb, Eugene. *Samuel Beckett: A Study of His Novels.* Seattle: Univ. of Washington Press; London: Peter Owen, 1970.
Wellershoff, Dieter. "Failure of an Attempt at De-Mythologization: Samuel Beckett's Novels." Trans. Martin Esslin. In *Samuel Beckett: A Collection of Critical Essays.* Ed. Martin Esslin. Englewood Cliffs, N.J.: Prentice-Hall, 1965, pp. 92-107.
Winston, Mathew. "*Watt's* First Footnote." *Journal of Modern Literautre*, 6 (February 1977), 69-82.
Worth, Katharine, ed. *Beckett the Shape Changer: A Symposium.* Boston: Routledge and Kegan Paul, 1975.
Zeltner-Neukomm, Gerda. *Das Wagnis des französischen Gegenwartromans: Die neue Welterfahrung in der Literatur.* Hamburg: Rowohlt, 1960.

Other Critical and Theoretical Studies

Where English translations of the French texts consulted are available, I have given the information immediately following the French entry.

Alter, Jean. *La Vision du monde d'Alain Robbe-Grillet: Structures et significations.* Geneva: Droz, 1966.

L'Analyse structurale du récit. Communications, 8 (1966).

Augustine, Saint. *The Confessions.* Trans. John K. Ryan. Garden City, N. Y.: Doubleday, 1960.

Axelos, Kostas. "Planetary Interlude." Trans. from the French by Sally Hess. In *Game, Play, Literature.* Ed. Jacques Ehrmann. *Yale French Studies,* No. 41 (1968), pp. 6-18.

Bachelard, Gaston. *L'Eau et les rêves: Essai sur l'imagination de la matière.* Paris: Corti, 1942./*Water and Dreams.* Trans. Edith Rodgers Farrell. Diss. Univ. of Iowa. Ann Arbor: University Microfilms, 1974.

———. *La Psychanalyse du feu.* Paris: Gallimard, 1949./*The Psychoanalysis of Fire.* Trans. Alan C. M. Ross. Boston: Beacon Press, 1964.

Bär, Eugen S. "Semiotic Model Theory in Psychoanalysis." *Semiotica,* 26 (1979), 99-119.

Barthes, Roland. "L'Effet de réel." *Communications,* 11 (1968), 84-89.

———. *S/Z.* Paris: Seuil, 1970./*S/Z.* Trans. Richard Miller. New York: Hill and Wang, 1974.

———. *Le Plaisir du texte.* Paris: Seuil, 1973./*The Pleasure of the Text.* Trans. Richard Miller. New York: Hill and Wang, 1975.

———. *Leçon.* Paris: Seuil, 1978.

Bateson, Gregory. *Steps to an Ecology of Mind.* New York: Ballantine, 1972.

Beaujour, Michel. "The Game of Poetics." In *Game, Play, Literature.* Ed. Jacques Ehrmann. *Yale French Studies,* No. 41 (1968), pp. 58-67.

Benveniste, Emile. *Problèmes de linguistique générale.* Paris: Gallimard, 1966./*Problems in General Linguistics.* Trans. Mary Elizabeth Meek. Coral Gables, Fla.: Univ. of Miami Press, 1971.

Bonaventura, Saint. *The Mind's Road to God.* Trans. George Boas. New York: Liberal Arts Press, 1953.

Both, Wayne C. *The Rhetoric of Fiction.* Chicago: Univ. of Chicago Press, 1961.

Brown, Norman O. *Life against Death: The Psychoanalytical Meaning of History.* Middletown, Conn.: Wesleyan Univ. Press, 1959.

Burnet, John. *Early Greek Philosophy.* 4th ed. 1930; rpt. London: Adam and Charles Black, 1963.

Butor, Michel. *Essais sur le roman.* Paris: Gallimard, Idées, 1975.

Caillois, Roger. *Les Jeux et les hommes: Le Masque et le vertige.* 2nd ed. Paris: Gallimard, Idées, 1967./ *Man, Play, and Games.* Trans. Meyer Barash. New York: Free Press of Glencoe, 1961.

Campbell, Joseph. "Bios and Mythos: Prolegomena to a Science of Mythology." In *Psychoanalysis and Culture.* Eds. G. B. Wilbur and M. Muensterberger. New York: International Universities Press, 1951, pp. 329-43. Rpt. in *Myth and Literature: Contemporary Theory and Practice.* Ed. John B. Vickery. Lincoln: Univ. of Nebraska Press, 1966, pp. 15-23.

———. *The Hero with a Thousand Faces.* 2nd ed. Princeton: Princeton Univ. Press, 1968.

Chatman, Seymour. "The Structure of Narrative Transmission." In *Style and Structure in Literature: Essays in the New Stylistics.* Ed. Roger Fowler. Ithaca: Cornell Univ. Press, 1975, pp. 213-57.

Chomsky, Noam. *Reflections on Language*. New York: Pantheon, 1975.
Cohn, Dorrit. *Transparent Minds: Narrative Modes for Presenting Consciousness in Fiction*. Princeton: Princeton Univ. Press, 1978.
Copi, Irving M. *The Theory of Logical Types*. London: Routledge and Kegan Paul, 1971.
Culler, Jonathan. *Structuralist Poetics: Structuralism, Linguistics and the Study of Literature*. Ithaca: Cornell Univ. Press, 1975.
Dällenbach, Lucien. *Le Récit spéculaire: Essai sur la mise en abyme*. Paris: Seuil, 1977.
Delcourt, Marie. *Oedipe ou la légende du conquérant*. Liège: Faculté de Philosophie et Lettres; Paris: Droz, 1944.
———. *Hermaphrodite: Mythes et rites de la bisexualité dans l'Antiquité classique*. Paris: Presses Universitaires de France, 1958./*Hermaphrodite: Myths and Rites of the Bisexual Figure in Classical Antiquity*. Trans. Jennifer Nicholson. London: Studio Books, 1961.
Deleuze, Gilles. *Présentation de Sacher-Masoch: Le Froid et le cruel. Avec le texte intégral de "La Vénus à la fourrure."* Paris: Minuit, 1967; 10/18, 1971./*Masochism: An Interpretation of Coldness and Cruelty. Together with the Entire Text of "Venus in Furs," by Leopold von Sacher-Masoch*. Trans. Jean McNeil. New York: G. Braziller, 1971.
———. *Proust et les signes*. 2nd ed. Paris: Presses Universitaires de France, 1970/*Proust and Signs*. Trans. Richard Howard. New York: G. Braziller, 1972.
———, and Félix Guattari. *Capitalisme et schizophrénie: L'Anti-Oedipe*. Paris: Minuit, 1972/*Capitalism and Schizophrenia: Anti-Oedipus*. Trans. Robert Hurley, et al. New York: Viking, 1977.
De Man, Paul. *Blindness and Insight: Essays in the Rhetoric of Contemporary Criticism*. New York: Oxford Univ. Press, 1971.
Derrida, Jacques. *L'Ecriture et la différence*. Paris: Seuil, 1967./*Writing and Difference*. Trans. Alan Bass. Chicago: Univ. of Chicago Press, 1978. (For "Freud and the Scene of Writing," I have used the translation by Jeffrey Mehlman in *Yale French Studies*, No. 48 [1972], pp. 73-117.)
———. *La Voix et le phénomène: Introduction au problème du signe dans la phénoménologie de Husserl*. Paris: Presses Universitaires de France, 1967./*Speech and Phenomena, and Other Essays on Husserl's Theory of Signs*. Trans. David B. Allison. Evanston: Northwestern Univ. Press, 1973.
———. *La Dissémination*. Paris: Seuil, 1972.
Descartes, René. *Œuvres et Lettres*. Bibliothèque de la Pleiade. Paris: Gallimard, 1953./*Philosophical Works*. 2 vols. Trans. Elizabeth S. Haldane and G. R. T. Ross. 1911; rpt. Cambridge: At the University Press, 1967.
Donato, Eugenio. "Of Structuralism and Literature." *MLN*, 82 (1967), 549-74.
———. "The Two Languages of Criticism." In *The Structuralist Controversy: The Languages of Criticism and the Sciences of Man*. Ed. Richard Macksey and Eugenio Donato. Baltimore: Johns Hopkins Univ. Press, 1970.
———. "The Shape of Fiction: Notes towards a Possible Classification of Narrative Discourses." *MLN*, 86 (1971), 807-22.

Donato, Eugenio. "Structuralism: The Aftermath." *Sub-Stance*, No. 7 (Fall 1973), pp. 9-26.

Dubois, Jean, et al. *Rhétorique générale*. Paris: Larousse, 1970.

Ducrot, Oswald, and Tzvetan Todorov. *Dictionnaire encyclopédique des sciences du langage*. Paris: Seuil, 1972./*Encyclopedic Dictionary of the Sciences of Language*. Trans. Catherine Porter. Baltimore: Johns Hopkins Univ. Press, 1979.

DuVerlie, Claud. "*Amor interruptus:* The Question of Eroticism or, Eroticism in Question in the Works of Claude Simon." Trans. from the French by J. Dickson. *Sub-Stance*, No. 8 (Winter 1974), pp. 21-33.

Ehrenzweig, Anton. *The Hidden Order of Art: A Study in the Psychology of Artistic Imagination*. Berkeley: Univ. of California Press, 1967.

Ehrmann, Jacques. "Homo Ludens Revisited." In *Game, Play, Literature*. Ed. Jacques Ehrmann. *Yale French Studies*. No. 41 (1968), pp. 31-57.

———. "Sur le jeu et l'origine, où il est surtout question de 'La dissémination' de Jacques Derrida." *Sub-Stance*, No. 7 (Fall 1973), pp. 113-23.

Ellmann, Richard. *James Joyce*. New York: Oxford Univ. Press, 1959.

Erickson, John D., ed. *Narrative Structure and Narratology. L'Esprit Créateur*, 17 (Fall 1977).

Fink, Eugen. "The Oasis of Happiness: Toward an Ontology of Play." Trans. form the German by Ute and Thomas Saine. In *Game, Play, Literature*. Ed. Jacques Ehrmann. *Yale French Studies*, No. 41 (1968), pp. 19-30.

Foucault, Michel. *Les Mots et les choses: Une Archéologie des sciences humaines*. Paris: Gallimard, 1966./*The Order of Things: An Archeology of the Human Sciences*. New York: Pantheon, 1970.

———. "Qu'est-ce qu'un auteur." *Bulletin de la Société Française de Philosophie*, 63 (1969), 73-104./"What Is an Author." in *Language, Counter-Memory, Practice: Selected Essays and Interviews*. Trans. Donald F. Bouchard and Sherry Simon. Ithaca: Cornell Univ. Press, 1977, pp. 113-38.

———. *L'Archéologie du savoir*. Paris: Gallimard, 1969./*The Archeology of Knowledge*. Trans. A. M. Sheridan Smith. New York: Pantheon, 1972.

———. *L'Ordre du discours*. Paris: Gallimard, 1971./*The Discourse on Language*. In *The Archeology of Knowledge*. New York: Pantheon, 1972.

Frank, Manfred. "The Infinite Text." Trans. Michael Schwerin. *Glyph*, 7 (1980), 70-101.

Freud, Sigmund. *The Interpretation of Dreams* (1900). Vols. IV and V of *The Standard Edition of the Complete Psychological Works*. Trans. James Strachey. London: Hogarth Press, 1953.

———. *Jokes and Their Relation to the Unconscious* (1905). Vol. VIII of *The Standard Edition*. London: Hogarth Press, 1960.

———. *Leonardo da Vinci and Memory of His Childhood* (1910). In Vol. XI of *The Standard Edition*. London: Hogarth Press, 1957.

———. "On Narcissism: An Introduction" (1914). In Vol. XIV of *The Standard Edition*. London: Hogarth Press, 1957.

———. *Papers on Metapsychology* (1915). In Vol. XIV of *The Standard Edition*. London: Hogarth, 1957.

Freud, Sigmund. *Beyond the Pleasure Principle* (1920). In Vol. XVIII of *The Standard Edition*. London: Hogarth Press, 1955.

———. "The Economic Problem of Masochism" (1924). In *Collected Papers*. Trans. Joan Riviere. New York: Basic Books, 1959. Vol. II.

Frye, Northrop. *Anatomy of Criticism: Four Essays*. Princeton: Princeton Univ. Press, 1957.

Gear, Maria Carmen, and Ernesto Cesar Liendo, and in collaboration with Luis J. Prieto. *Sémiologie psychanalytique*. Trans. from the Spanish by Marie Tulien and Daniel Glauser. Paris: Minuit, 1975.

Genette, Gérard. *Figures*. Paris: Seuil, 1966.

———. "Frontières du récit." *Communication*, 8 (1966), 152-63. Rpt. in *Figures II*. Paris: Seuil, 1969, pp. 49-69./"Boundaries of Narrative." Trans. Ann Levonas. *New Literary History*, 8, No. 1 (1976), 1-13.

———. *Figures III*. Paris: Seuil, 1972/*Narrative Discourse: An Essay in Method*. Trans. Jane E. Lewin. Ithaca: Cornell Univ. Press, 1980.

Girard, René. *Mensonge romantique et vérité romanesque*. Paris: Grasset, 1961./*Deceit, Desire, and the Novel: Self and Other in Literary Structure*. Trans. Yvonne Freccero. Baltimore: Johns Hopkins Press, 1965.

———. "De l'expérience romanesque au mythe oedipien." *Critique*, No. 222 (1965), pp. 899-924.

———. "Symétrie et dissymétrie dans le mythe d'Oedipe." *Critique*, No. 249 (1968), pp. 99-135.

———. *La Violence et le sacré*. Paris: Grasset, 1972./*Violence and the Sacred*. Trans. Patrick Gregory. Baltimore: Johns Hopkins University Press, 1977.

———. *Des choses cachées depuis la fondation du monde*. Paris: Grasset, 1978.

Green, André. "Répétition, différence, réplication: En relisant *Au delà du principe de plaisir*." *Revue Française de Psychanalyse*, 34 (1970), 461-501.

Harari, Josué, ed. *Textual Strategies: Perspectives in Post-Structuralist Criticism*. Ithaca: Cornell Univ. Press, 1979.

Heath, Stephen. *The Nouveau Roman: A Study in the Practice of Writing*. London: Elek, 1972.

Hendricks, William O. "Methodology of Narrative Structural Analysis." *Semiotica*, 7 (1973), 163-84.

Jacobson, Richard. "Absence, Authority, and the Text." *Glyph*, 3 (1978), 137-47.

Jakobson, Roman. "Two Aspects of Language and Two Types of Aphasic Disturbances." 1956; rpt. in *Selected Writings*. Vol. II. The Hague: Mouton, 1971, 239-59.

———. "Shifters, Verbal Categories, and the Russian Verb." Cambridge, Mass., 1957; rpt. in *Selected Writings*. Vol. II. The Hague: Mouton, 1971, 130-47.

———. "Closing Statements: Linguistics and Poetics." In *Style in Language*. Ed. Thomas A. Sebeok. Cambridge, Mass.: M. I. T. Press, 1960, pp. 350-77.

Jameson, Fredric. *The Prison-House of Language: A Critical Account of Structuralism and Russian Formalism*. Princeton: Princeton Univ. Press, 1972.

Joos, Martin. *The Five Clocks*. New York: Harcourt Brace and World, 1967.

Jung, Carl G. *Symbols of Transformation: An Analysis of the Prelude to a Case of Schizophrenia.* 2nd ed. Vol. V of the *Collected Works.* Trans. R. F. C. Hull. Princeton: Princeton Univ. Press, 1967.

———. *Analytical Psychology, Its Theory and Practice: The Tavistock Lectures.* New York: Pantheon, 1968.

Klein, Melanie. *Love, Guilt and Reparation and Other Works, 1921-45.* London: Hogarth Press, 1975.

———. *Envy and Gratitude and Other Works, 1946-1963.* [New York]: Delacorte Press, 1975.

Kristeva, Julia. *La Révolution du langage poétique: L'Avant-garde à la fin du XIXe siècle; Lautréamont et Mallarmé.* Paris: Seuil, 1974.

Lacan, Jacques. *Ecrits.* Paris: Seuil, 1966./"The Function of Language in Psychoanalysis." In *The Language of the Self.* Trans. Anthony Wilden. Baltimore: Johns Hopkins Press, 1968, pp. 3-87; and *Ecrits: A Selection.* Trans. Alan Sheridan. New York: Norton, 1977.

———. "Of Structure as an Inmixing of an Otherness Prerequisite to Any Subject Whatever." In *The Structuralist Controversy: The Language of Criticism and the Sciences of Man.* Ed. Richard Macksey and Eugenio Donato. Baltimore: Johns Hopkins Univ. Press, 1970, pp. 186-95.

Laplanche, Jean, and J.-B. Pontalis. *Vocabulaire de la psychanalyse.* Paris: Presses Universitaires de France, 1967./*The Language of Psychoanalysis.* Trans. Donald Nicholson-Smith. New York: Norton, 1973.

Leech, Geoffrey N. *A Linguistic Guide to English Poetry.* London: Longmans, 1969.

Le Galliot, Jean, et al. *Psychanalyse et langages littéraires: Théorie et pratique.* Paris: Nathan, 1977.

Lemaire, Anika. *Jacques Lacan.* 2nd ed. Brussels: Pierre Mardaga, 1977.

Lévi-Strauss, Claude. *Anthropologie structurale.* Paris: Plon, 1958./*Structural Anthropology.* Trans. Claire Jacobson and Brooke Grundfest Schoepf. New York: Basic Books, 1963.

———. *Le Cru et le cuit.* Vol. I of *Mythologiques.* Paris: Plon, 1964./ *The Raw and the Cooked.* Trans. John and Doreen Weightman. New York: Harper and Row, 1969.

———. *L'Homme nu.* Vol. IV of *Mythologiques.* Paris: Plon, 1971.

Levinas, Emmanuel. *Totalité et infini: Essai sur l'extériorité.* 4th ed. The Hague: Martinus Nijhoff, 1974./*Totality and Infinity: An Essay on Exteriority.* Trans. Alphonso Lingis. Pittsburgh: Duquesne Univ. Press, 1969.

Lukács, Georg. *The Meaning of Contemporary Realism.* Trans. from the German by John and Necke Mander. London: Merlin Press, 1962.

Lyons, John. *Semantics.* Cambridge: Cambridge Univ. Press, 1977. Vol. II.

Macksey, Richard, and Eugenio Donato, eds. *The Stucturalist Controversy: The Languages of Criticism and the Sciences of Man.* Baltimore: Johns Hopkins Univ. Press, 1970.

———. "Lions and Squares: Opening Remarks." In *The Structuralist Controversy,* pp. 1-14.

Mallarmé, Stéphane. *Œuvres complètes.* Bibliothèque de la Pléiade. Paris: Gallimard, 1945./*Mallarmé: Selected Prose Poems, Essays, and Letters.* Trans. Bradford Cook. Baltimore: Johns Hopkins Press, 1956.

Mannoni, Octave. *Freud.* Ecrivains de Toujours. Paris: Seuil, 1968./*Freud.* Trans. Renaud Bruce. New York: Pantheon, 1971.

Marcuse, Herbert. *Eros and Civilization: A Philosophical Inquiry into Freud.* 1955; rpt. Boston: Beacon Press, 1966.

Marin, Louis. "*Puss-in-Boots:* Power of Signs — Signs of Power." *Diacritics,* 7 (Summer 1977), 54-63.

Mehlman, Jeffrey, ed. *French Freud: Structural Studies in Psychoanalysis. Yale French Studies,* No. 48 (1972).

Millar, Susanna. *The Psychology of Play.* Middlesex: Penguin, 1968.

Miller, J. Hillis. "Ariadne's Thread: Repetition and the Narrative Line." *Critical Inquiry,* 3 (Autumn 1976), 57-77.

Morrissette, Bruce. "Clefs pour *Les Gommes.*" In *Les Gommes.* By Alain Robbe-Grillet. Paris: Union Générale d'Editions, 10/18, 1962, pp. 269-314./Rev. version in *The Novels of Robbe-Grillet.* Trans. by the author. Ithaca: Cornell Univ. Press, 1975, pp. 38-74.

―――. "Games and Game Structures in Robbe-Grillet." In *Game, Play, Literature.* Ed. Jacques Ehrmann. *Yale French Studies,* No. 41 (1968), pp. 159-67.

Nadeau, Maurice. *Le Roman français depuis la guerre.* Paris: Gallimard, 1963./*The French Novel since the War.* Trans. A. M. Sheridan Smith. New York: Grove Press, 1969.

Nietzsche, Friedrich. *Philosophy during the Tragic Age of the Greeks.* Vol. II of *The Complete Works.* Trans. Maximilian A. Mügge. 1909-11; rpt. New York: Russell and Russell, 1964.

―――. *Das Philosophenbuch: Theoretische Studien.* Bilingual German-French edition. Ed. and trans. Angèle K. Marietti. Paris: Aubier-Flammarion, 1969./*Philosophy and Truth: Selections from Nietzsche's Notebooks of the Early 1870's.* Ed. and trans. Daniel Breazeale. Atlantic Highlands, N. J.: Humanities Press, 1979.

Ohmann, Richard. "Speech, Action, and Style." In *Literary Style: A Symposium.* Ed. Seymour Chatman. New York: Oxford Univ. Press, 1971, pp. 241-59.

Rapport, Anatol. "What Is Semantics?" *American Scientist* (Jan. 1952). Rpt. in *Classics in Semantics.* Ed. Donald E. Hayden and E. Paul Alworth. New York: Philosophical Library, 1965, pp. 337-54.

Reed, Arden. "Abysmal Influence: Baudelaire, Coleridge, De Quincey, Piranesi, Wordsworth." *Glyph,* 4 (1978), 189-206.

Reik, Theodor. *Dogma and Compulsion: Psychoanalytic Studies of Religion and Myths.* Trans. Bernard Miall. New York: International Universities Press, 1951.

Ricardou, Jean. *Le Nouveau Roman.* Ecrivains de Toujours, No. 92. Paris: Seuil, 1973.

Robbe-Grillet, Alain. *Pour un nouveau roman.* Paris: Minuit, 1963./*For a New Novel: Essays on Fiction.* Trans. Richard Howard. New York: Grove Press, 1965.

Russell, Bertrand. *Principles of Mathematics.* 2nd ed. New York: W. W. Norton, 1938.

―――, and Alfred N. Whitehead. *Principia Mathematica.* Vol I. 2nd ed. 1925; rpt. Cambridge, Eng.: Univ. Press, Paperback Edition to *56, 1962.

Scholes, Robert. *Structuralism in Literature: An Introduction.* New Haven: Yale Univ. Press, 1974.

Spivak, Gayatri Chakravorty. "Translator's Preface." In *Of Grammatology*. By Jacques Derrida. Baltimore: Johns Hopkins Univ. Press, 1974, pp. ix-xc.

Stewart, Susan. *Nonsense: Aspects of Intertextuality in Folklore and Literature*. Baltimore: Johns Hopkins Univ. Press, 1978.

Sullivan, Dennis G. "On Vision in Proust: The Icon and the *Voyeur*." *MLN*, 84 (1969), 646-61.

Todorov, Tzvetan ed. and trans. *Théorie de la littérature: Textes des formalistes russes*. Paris: Seuil, 1965.

———. *Poétique de la prose*. Paris: Seuil, 1971./*The Poetics of Prose*. Trans. Richard Howard. Ithaca: Cornell Univ. Press, 1977.

Traugott, Elizabeth Closs. "Spatial Expressions of Tense and Temporal Sequencing: A Contribution to the Study of Semantic Fields." *Semiotica*, 15 (1975), 207-30.

———, and Mary Louise Pratt. *Linguistics for Students of Literature*. New York: Harcourt Brace Jovanovich, 1980.

Vickery, John B., ed. *Myth and Literature: Contemporary Theory and Practice*. Lincoln: Univ. of Nebraska Press, 1966.

Whorf, Benjamin Lee. *Language, Thought and Reality* (1940). Rpt. in *Selected Writings of Benjamin Lee Whorf*. Ed. John B. Carroll. Cambridge, Mass.: MIT Press, 1956.

Wilden, Anthony. *The Language of the Self*. Baltimore: Johns Hopkins Press, 1968.

Wimsatt, William. "How to Compose Chess Problems, and Why." In *Game, Play, Literature*. Ed. Jacques Ehrmann. *Yale French Studies*, No. 41 (1968), pp. 68-85.

Wood, Barbara S. *Children and Communication: Verbal and Nonverbal Language Development*. Englewood Cliffs, N. J.: Prentice-Hall, 1976.

NORTH CAROLINA STUDIES IN THE ROMANCE LANGUAGES AND LITERATURES

I.S.B.N. Prefix 0-8078-

Recent Titles

ESTUDIOS DE LITERATURA HISPANOAMERICANA EN HONOR A JOSÉ J. ARROM, edited by Andrew P. Debicki and Enrique Pupo-Walker. 1975. (Symposia, No. 2). -952-9.
MEDIEVAL MANUSCRIPTS AND TEXTUAL CRITICISM, edited by Christopher Kleinhenz. 1976. (Symposia, No. 4). -954-5.
SAMUEL BECKETT. THE ART OF RHETORIC, edited by Edouard Morot-Sir, Howard Harper, and Dougald McMillan III. 1976. (Symposia, No. 5). -955-3.
DELIE. CONCORDANCE, by Jerry Nash. 1976. 2 Volumes. (No. 174).
FIGURES OF REPETITION IN THE OLD PROVENÇAL LYRIC: A STUDY IN THE STYLE OF THE TROUBADOURS, by Nathaniel B. Smith. 1976. (No. 176). -9176-2.
A CRITICAL EDITION OF LE REGIME TRESUTILE ET TRESPROUFITABLE POUR CONSERVER ET GARDER LA SANTE DU CORPS HUMAIN, by Patricia Willett Cummins. 1977. (No. 177).
THE DRAMA OF SELF IN GUILLAUME APOLLINAIRE'S "ALCOOLS", by Richard Howard Stamelman. 1976. (No. 178). -9178-9.
A CRITICAL EDITION OF "LA PASSION NOSTRE SEIGNEUR" FROM MANUSCRIPT 1131 FROM THE BIBLIOTHEQUE SAINTE-GENEVIEVE, PARIS, by Edward J. Gallagher. 1976. (No. 179). -9179-7.
A QUANTITATIVE AND COMPARATIVE STUDY OF THE VOCALISM OF THE LATIN INSCRIPTIONS OF NORTH AFRICA, BRITAIN, DALMATIA, AND THE BALKANS, by Stephen William Omeltchenko. 1977. (No. 180). -9180-0.
OCTAVIEN DE SAINT-GELAIS "LE SEJOUR D'HONNEUR", edited by Joseph A. James. 1977. (No. 181). -9181-9.
A STUDY OF NOMINAL INFLECTION IN LATIN INSCRIPTIONS, by Paul A. Gaeng. 1977. (No. 182). -9182-7.
THE LIFE AND WORKS OF LUIS CARLOS LÓPEZ, by Martha S. Bazik. 1977. (No. 183). -9183-5.
"THE CORT D'AMOR". A THIRTEENTH-CENTURY ALLEGORICAL ART OF LOVE, by Lowanne E. Jones. 1977. (No. 185). -9185-1.
PHYTONYMIC DERIVATIONAL SYSTEMS IN THE ROMANCE LANGUAGES: STUDIES IN THEIR ORIGIN AND DEVELOPMENT, by Walter E. Geiger. 1978. (No. 187). -9187-8.
LANGUAGE IN GIOVANNI VERGA'S EARLY NOVELS, by Nicholas Patruno. 1977. (No. 188). -9188-6.
BLAS DE OTERO EN SU POESÍA, by Moraima de Semprún Donahue. 1977. (No. 189). -9189-4.
LA ANATOMÍA DE "EL DIABLO COJUELO": DESLINDES DEL GÉNERO ANATOMÍSTICO, por C. George Peale. 1977. (No. 191). -9191-6.
RICHARD SANS PEUR, EDITED FROM "LE ROMANT DE RICHART" AND FROM GILLES CORROZET'S "RICHART SANS PAOUR", by Denis Joseph Conlon. 1977. (No. 192). -9192-4.
MARCEL PROUST'S GRASSET PROOFS. *Commentary and Variants,* by Douglas Alden. 1978. (No. 193). -9193-2.
MONTAIGNE AND FEMINISM, by Cecile Insdorf. 1977. (No. 194). -9194-0.
SANTIAGO F. PUGLIA, AN EARLY PHILADELPHIA PROPAGANDIST FOR SPANISH AMERICAN INDEPENDENCE, by Merle E. Simmons. 1977. (No. 195). -9195-9.
BAROQUE FICTION-MAKING. A STUDY OF GOMBERVILLE'S "POLEXANDRE", by Edward Baron Turk. 1978. (No. 196). -9196-7.
THE TRAGIC FALL: DON ÁLVARO DE LUNA AND OTHER FAVORITES IN SPANISH GOLDEN AGE DRAMA, by Raymond R. MacCurdy. 1978. (No. 197). -9197-5.

When ordering please cite the *ISBN Prefix* plus the last four digits for each title.

Send orders to: University of North Carolina Press
Chapel Hill
North Carolina 27514
U. S. A.

NORTH CAROLINA STUDIES IN THE ROMANCE LANGUAGES AND LITERATURES

I.S.B.N. Prefix 0-8078-

Recent Titles

A BAHIAN HERITAGE. An Ethnolinguistic Study of African Influences on Bahian Portuguese, by William W. Megenney. 1978. (No. 198). *-9198-3.*
"LA QUERELLE DE LA ROSE: Letters and Documents", by Joseph L. Baird and John R. Kane. 1978. (No. 199). *-9199-1.*
TWO AGAINST TIME. A Study of the Very Present Worlds of Paul Claudel and Charles Péguy, by Joy Nachod Humes. 1978. (No. 200). *-9200-9.*
TECHNIQUES OF IRONY IN ANATOLE FRANCE. Essay on *Les Sept Femmes de la Barbe-Bleue*, by Diane Wolfe Levy. 1978. (No. 201). *-9201-7.*
THE PERIPHRASTIC FUTURES FORMED BY THE ROMANCE REFLEXES OF "VADO (AD)" "PLUS INFINITIVE, by James Joseph Champion. 1978 (No. 202). *-9202-5.*
THE EVOLUTION OF THE LATIN /b/-/ṷ/ MERGER: A Quantitative and Comparative Analysis of the *B-V* Alternation in Latin Inscriptions, by Joseph Louis Barbarino. 1978 (No. 203). *-9203-3.*
METAPHORIC NARRATION: THE STRUCTURE AND FUNCTION OF METAPHORS IN "A LA RECHERCHE DU TEMPS PERDU", by Inge Karalus Crosman. 1978 (No. 204). *-9204-1.*
LE VAIN SIECLE GUERPIR. A Literary Approach to Sainthood through Old French Hagiography of the Twelfth Century, by Phyllis Johnson and Brigitte Cazelles. 1979. (No. 205). *-9205-X.*
THE POETRY OF CHANGE: A STUDY OF THE SURREALIST WORKS OF BENJAMIN PÉRET, by Julia Field Costich. 1979. (No. 206). *-9206-8.*
NARRATIVE PERSPECTIVE IN THE POST-CIVIL WAR NOVELS OF FRANCISCO AYALA "MUERTES DE PERRO" AND "EL FONDO DEL VASO", by Maryellen Bieder. 1979. (No. 207). *-9207-6.*
RABELAIS: HOMO LOGOS, by Alice Fiola Berry. 1979. (No. 208). *-9208-4.*
"DUEÑAS" AND "DONCELLAS": A STUDY OF THE "DOÑA RODRÍGUEZ" EPISODE IN "DON QUIJOTE", by Conchita Herdman Marianella. 1979. (No. 209). *-9209-2.*
PIERRE BOAISTUAU'S "HISTOIRES TRAGIQUES": A STUDY OF NARRATIVE FORM AND TRAGIC VISION, by Richard A. Carr. 1979. (No. 210). *-9210-6.*
REALITY AND EXPRESSION IN THE POETRY OF CARLOS PELLICER, by George Melnykovich. 1979. (No. 211). *-9211-4.*
MEDIEVAL MAN, HIS UNDERSTANDING OF HIMSELF, HIS SOCIETY, AND THE WORLD, by Urban T. Holmes, Jr. 1980. (No. 212). *-9212-2.*
MÉMOIRES SUR LA LIBRAIRIE ET SUR LA LIBERTÉ DE LA PRESSE, introduction and notes by Graham E. Rodmell. 1979. (No. 213). *-9213-0.*
THE FICTIONS OF THE SELF. THE EARLY WORKS OF MAURICE BARRES, by Gordon Shenton. 1979. (No. 214). *-9214-9.*
CECCO ANGIOLIERI. A STUDY, by Gifford P. Orwen. 1979. (No. 215). *-9215-7.*
THE INSTRUCTIONS OF SAINT LOUIS: A CRITICAL TEXT, by David O'Connell. 1979. (No. 216). *-9216-5.*
ARTFUL ELOQUENCE, JEAN LEMAIRE DE BELGES AND THE RHETORICAL TRADITION, by Michael F. O. Jenkins. 1980 (No. 217). *-9217-3.*
A CONCORDANCE TO MARIVAUX'S COMEDIES IN PROSE, edited by Donald C. Spinelli. 1979 (No. 218). 4 volumes, *-9218-1* (set); *-9219-X* (v. 1); *-9220-3* (v. 2); *-9221-1* (v. 3); *-9222-X* (v. 4.)
ABYSMAL GAMES IN THE NOVELS OF SAMUEL BECKETT, by Angela B. Moorjani. 1982 (No. 219). *-9223-8.*

When ordering please cite the *ISBN Prefix* plus the last four digits for each title.

Send orders to: University of North Carolina Press
Chapel Hill
North Carolina 27514
U. S. A.

ERRATA

MOORJANI, Angela B. *Abysmal Games in the Novels of Samuel Beckett*. North Carolina Studies in the Romance Languages and Literatures, Number 219.

Page	Error	Correction
1. p. 20, n. 10, last line	pp. 197-14	pp. 107-14
2. p. 27, n. 6, l. 15	Millier	Miller
3. p. 29, end of first paragraph	from one polyphonous level to the text	to the next
4. p. 45, l. 14	productions becomes	become
5. p. 55, second line from bottom	"Je viens d'écrire. Je crois...	"Je viens d'écrire, Je crois...
6. p. 67, l. 13	ronudelay	roundelay
7. p. 79, l. 9	*for/da*	*fort/da*
8. p. 81, l. 2	parallel protagonist's	parallel the protagonist's
9. p. 83, l. 12	ludricrous	ludicrous
10. p. 90, n. 32	*Language et fiction*	*Langage et fiction*
11. p. 91, l. 16	word without grace	world without grace
12. p. 91, 5th line from bottom	that is must remain	that it must remain
13. p. 91, last line	similarly comes	similarly come
14. p. 97, l. 16	adopts it inverted ...form	adopts its inverted ...form
15. p. 107, 6th line from bottom	matatextual	metatextual
16. p. 107, n. 51, l. 5	Tafliaferri	Tagliaferri
17. p. 132, 7th line from bottom	no other voice than the narrators'	the narrator's
18. p. 137, last line	repetedly	repeatedly
19. p. 140, l. 15	Connolloy's	Connolly's
20. p. 142, segment 3, l. 1	As the end of the day	At the end of the day

Page	Error	Correction
21. p. 147, l. 6	stage meeting	stage meetings
22. p. 159, 9th line from bottom	*Journal of Modern Literautre*	*Journal of Modern Literature*
23. p. 160	Both, Wayne C.	Booth, Wayne C.
24. p. 162, 6th line from bottom	*Leonardo da Vinci and Memory of His Childhood*	*Leonardo da Vinci and a Memory...*
25. p. 164, l. 17	*The Structuralist Controversy: The Language of Criticism*	*The Structuralist Controversy: The Languages...*
26. p. 164	Levinas, Emmanuel	Lévinas, Emmanuel
27. p. 165	Rapport, Anatol	Rapoport, Anatol

The Department of Romance Studies Digital Arts and Collaboration Lab at the University of North Carolina at Chapel Hill is proud to support the digitization of the North Carolina Studies in the Romance Languages and Literatures series.

www.ingramcontent.com/pod-product-compliance
Lightning Source LLC
Chambersburg PA
CBHW020417230426
43663CB00007BA/1200